Esquire
The Meaning of Life

Esquire

The Meaning of Life

(Wit, Wisdom, and
65 Wonder from
Extraordinary People)

Edited by Brendan Vaughan

HEARST BOOKS
A Division of Sterling Publishing Co, Inc.
New York

Copyright © 2004 Hearst Communications, Inc.

A Primrose Production
Designed by Lync/Lynne Yeamans

Library of Congress Cataloging-in-Publication Data

Esquire—the meaning of life : wit, wisdom, and wonder from 65 extraordinary people.
   p. cm.
  Includes index.
  ISBN 1-58816-261-3
  1. United States—Biography. 2. Biography—20th century. 3. Celebrities—United States—
Biography. 4. Entertainers—United States—Biography. 5. Intellectuals—United States—
Biography. 6. American wit and humor—20th century. 7. Meaning (Philosophy)—History—20th
century. 8. Popular culture—United States—History—20th century. 9. United States—Social life
and customs—20th century. I. Esquire, inc.
  CT220.E78 2004
  920.073—dc22

                                                                           2004047509

10 9 8 7 6 5

Published by Hearst Books
A Division of Sterling Publishing Co., Inc.
387 Park Avenue South, New York, NY 10016

Esquire and Hearst Books are trademarks of Hearst Communications, Inc.

www.esquire.com

Distributed in Canada by Sterling Publishing
C/o Canadian Manda Group, 165 Dufferin Street
Toronto, Ontario, Canada M6K 3H6

Distributed in Great Britain by Chrysalis Books Group PLC
The Chrysalis Building, Bramley Road, London W10 6SP, England

Distributed in Australia by Capricorn Link (Australia) Pty. Ltd.
P.O. Box 704, Windsor, NSW 2756 Australia

Printed in China

Sterling ISBN 13: 978-1-58816-261-8
        ISBN 10: 1-58816-261-3

"When listening to somebody, look him in the eye as if he is the only person in the world."

—CAL FUSSMAN, WHO CONDUCTED 25 OF THE 65 INTERVIEWS COLLECTED IN THIS BOOK

Contents

Introduction

It started in 1998 with Rod Steiger. I can't say with certainty whose idea "What I've Learned" was. But it's certain that Deputy Editor Peter Griffin came up with the name. It's certain that the first subject was legendary actor Rod Steiger. And it's equally certain that this collection of wisdom—65 classic "What I've Learned" interviews from the pages of *Esquire*—earns the title we've given it: *The Meaning of Life*.

Our concept from the start was to go to people who had lived a life. We wanted men and women who had triumphed and failed in equally conspicuous measure. We wanted people who had achieved great things and people who had offended us. We wanted heroes and bad guys. And then we wanted to pry their essential wisdom out of them.

Over the six years we've been publishing this column, there have been interviews that have lasted for up to seven hours. There have been interviews that have been as short as 45 minutes. In a couple of instances (legendary recluse Phil Spector and paranoid genius Garry Shandling), the subject wrote his own "What I've Learned"—and then rewrote and rewrote and rewrote. In nearly every case, the subject has embraced and even enjoyed the process. Sumner Redstone kept his jet waiting for a couple hours while he finished up with Cal Fussman. Fussman's interviews with Al Pacino stretched over dozens of hours during a two-week period. Near the end of 2003, Fussman interviewed business giant Jack Welch. After two and a half hours, Welch insisted on turning the tables and interviewing Fussman, and then Welch announced, "Come on, we're going to lunch!" The process varies but the result is nearly always the same. A life's wisdom, distilled.

But back to Steiger. *Esquire* writer at large Mike Sager had briefed him on what we were after. We want conclusions, he'd explained. We want to know what life has taught you. A couple days later, when Sager showed up at Steiger's home, Steiger was ready. He had filled page after page of a legal pad with maxims and aphorisms, most of which he had painstakingly crafted over the intervening two days.

This is why "What I've Learned" has become one of the most enduringly popular things we do at *Esquire*. It boils down an extraordinary person's essential experiences and reflections into an incredibly potent, easily digestible meal. It's funny and moving and filled with insight. It is the rare "What I've Learned" that hasn't lodged at least one nugget of wisdom in my brain forever. Some of my favorites:

Julia Child: "There is nothing worse than grilled vegetables."
Rodney Dangerfield: "Time and tide and hookers wait for no man."
F. Lee Bailey: "Laughing juries don't convict."
Peter Boyle: "Very few people know this: There's a Prada outlet store. But it's in Tuscany."
David Brown: "Bad dreams are more likely the result of strong cheeses than suppressed guilt."
Conrad Dobler: "If it flies, floats, or fucks, rent it."
Rip Torn: "I've never hit anybody who hasn't clocked me two or three times."

One of the frustrating things about magazine publishing is that even when we do memorable work, it's ephemeral. It's gone at the end of the month when the next issue hits the newsstand. We've always thought "What I've Learned" deserved to last, and we've also always wanted to have all these people in one place. I mean, can you imagine the conversation between legendary economist John Kenneth Galbraith and Gene Simmons, the lead singer of Kiss? What you have here is the next best thing. A collection of the conclusions of some of the most extraordinary and accomplished and inspirational and (in some cases) oddest people in the world.

With the publication of this book, "What I've Learned" will endure in a new format. Meanwhile, we'll continue to publish these memorable interviews every month in the magazine. And in another five years or so, we'll have enough for volume two.

DAVID GRANGER, EDITOR IN CHIEF

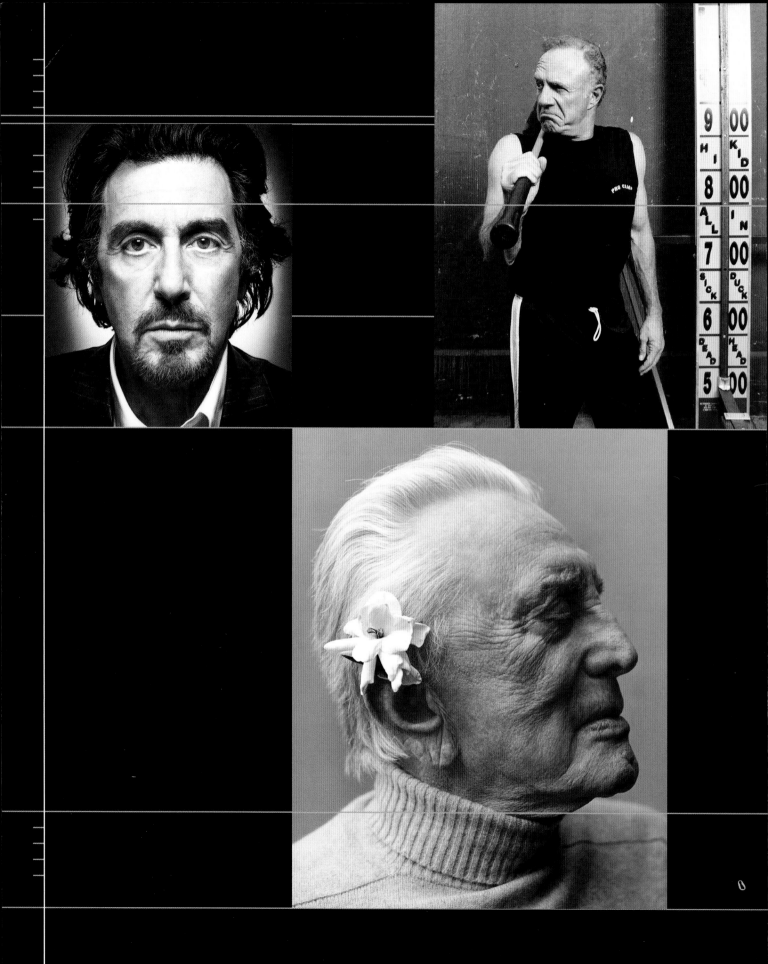

The
Characters

Peter Boyle

James Caan

Robert De Niro

Kirk Douglas

Faye Dunaway

Jack Nicholson

Al Pacino

Christopher Reeve

Rod Steiger

Rip Torn

Peter Boyle

People who really aren't bright become major executives. Don't quote me on that.

Well, you can quote me. *Some* people. I'm afraid. I'm not bulletproof. Nobody's untouchable.

Acting's very existential. It happens in the moment. The dilemma, the challenge to the actor, is to capture that moment again. If you try to capture that moment again, you're out of the moment.

Brando's the master.

I had an identity crisis, as a lot of teenagers do, and instead of joining the Army, instead of entering into an unfortunate marriage, instead of running away and joining the circus, I joined the Christian Brothers. The first year was very intense. It was like living in a medieval monastery: get up at five in the morning and pray for three hours, and then study, and then work, and then study, and then pray some more, and then work some more, and then go to sleep. At a certain point, it went from being very intense to being very difficult. I felt some deep spiritual connection. I also felt my own craziness. Exultation, up and down—I tend to be a little cyclic in terms of my moods. Does that sound familiar to anybody out there?

The idea of being celibate for life—I couldn't live up to it. I was having trouble with the celibacy issue, and I was in chapel praying, and I left the chapel, went into the common room, and turned on the TV to see Sheena of the Jungle—old black-and-white Sheena. I knew I was in trouble. Better get back to the chapel—Jesus is waiting. Sheena is my Mary Magdalene.

I had doubts. I had doubts in faith. I was twenty years old, which is a very hard time in anybody's life, I don't care what they say. Anybody who makes it through twenty and twenty-one is really tough.

We are animals. And we also are vegetables. I know because I watch television right in this room.

I always root for the character actor.

I knew when we were making the *Everybody Loves Raymond* pilot that it was really good. That almost seven years later I would be sitting here—I didn't know *that*. It's a really good show, and I really feel good about it. It makes me happy. It makes me less neurotic. It helps me. When I was a starving actor, life had no structure except suffer, suffer, suffer.

I have an ascot, but I've never worn it. You've gotta have panache. I can manage it if it's in a play—I can play a *character* with panache. But in everyday life, I wear a T-shirt and sneakers. Cary Grant, he had panache. Maybe Hugh Grant has it. Michael Caine doesn't have panache. Where can you find it? Is it on the Internet? It's something that's lacking in life nowadays.

When I was growing up, Roosevelt was, in our family, God. The greatest man who ever lived. But I think television's changed that. I mean, there hasn't been a candidate since Dwight Eisenhower who doesn't have a lot of hair.

Very few people know this: There's a Prada outlet store. But it's in Tuscany.

A friend of mine once said, "The moment of truth is a lie." He was being funny. I keep looking for it. I've had a few. But you can't explain it. It's deeply moving, and yet then when it's over, you're back in the street again, saying, What the hell happened? What the hell happened? What was that flash of light? I want it again.

Black guys can be reverends and have a lot of girlfriends and sing gospel. White guys gotta go into a monastery and never see a date for five years.

It's astonishing. In the name of God: the Inquisition, the Conquest, the Crusades, even the Japanese kamikaze pilots.

If Ed Sullivan can be a TV legend, it tells you something about TV.

When I was about to become a father, my friend Burgess Meredith said, "You're gonna find something wonderful—someone you love more than yourself." For self-centered people, it's a great blessing.

You see more life experience in one trip to the corner to buy the paper in New York than you do in a month in another place.

Life is not easy. The symbol of comedy and tragedy—the masks—means a lot more to me now that I'm older. There's less tragedy and more comedy in my life.

Whatever we lose, we'll get back.

INTERVIEWED BY SCOTT RAAB // Photograph by Michael Lewis

bio

BORN: Philadelphia, Pennsylvania
October 18, 1935

> Film highlights include roles in *Joe* (1970), *Young Frankenstein* (1974), *Taxi Driver* (1976), and *Monster's Ball* (2001).

> Since 1996, Boyle has starred as Ray Romano's father, Frank Barone, on CBS's *Everybody Loves Raymond*. He's received Emmy Award nominations for Outstanding Supporting Actor in a Comedy Series three times, in 1999, 2000, and 2001.
> The best man at Boyle's wedding was John Lennon.

James Caan

I'll bump into a guy in a bar, and he'll say, "I'm sorry, Sonny!" It's surreal.

Nobody should give a shit about an actor's opinion on politics.

One night I went over to get some dope from some Hollywood tough guy. After I left, my son Scott, who was only fifteen, went over with a baseball bat to kill him. I was laughing out of one eye and crying out of the other. I thought, Who am I kidding?

There's a big difference between wanting to work and having to work. And I had to learn that the hard way. Now money is very important to me, because I ain't got it.

You have to be very careful when you let someone win.

I'm sort of a Walter Mitty. I got fewer brain cells than most people, so when I got friendly with cowboys, I started rodeoing. When I was calf-roping, there was something about the dirt that made me feel clean.

Some guys say beauty is only skin deep. But when you walk into a party, you don't see somebody's brain. The initial contact has to be the sniffing.

Actors have bodyguards and entourages not because anybody wants to hurt them—who would want to hurt an actor?—but because they want to get recognized. God forbid someone doesn't recognize them. They'd have a fucking heart attack.

What's the difference between sex and love? I have four wives and five kids. I apparently don't know the difference.

For the record, I've never been in an orgy.

You're the only one who's closing your eyes at night. There's no one else who can do it for you.

There are a lot of guys in Hollywood who clap you on the back just a little too hard.

bio

BORN: Bronx, New York
March 26, 1939

> Best known for his Oscar–nominated performance as Sonny Corleone in *The Godfather* (1972) and his Emmy-nominated portrayal of football star Brian Piccolo in *Brian's Song* (1970). Recently he's appeared as Big Ed, chief of security at a casino, in NBC's series *Las Vegas*.

> Caan is almost as famous for the roles he turned down, which include McMurphy in *One Flew Over the Cuckoo's Nest*.

> Caan has participated in professional rodeos, earning him the nickname "The Jewish Cowboy." He also owns a stable of racehorses.

Showing up every day isn't enough. There are a lot of guys who show up every day who shouldn't have showed up at all.

I had great, great times as a Little League coach. People were talking about me quitting acting, and they would say, "What about your creative juices?" Coaching is creative, because you could take a kid who thought he wasn't any good and, within four minutes, change his mind. And I didn't have to wait six months for them to put music to it.

How good a Little League coach was I? I was a little hyper. One thing I learned was that talent comes from everywhere; it doesn't have to come just from the ghetto. But in Beverly Hills, because Daddy has a grocery store, the kids lack a lot of try.

I had my first puff on a joint when I was twenty-four and a half, and I was petrified. I thought I was gonna see elephants. Five, six years later, I'm in Hollywood. I got a little cocaine in my pocket, a couple of quaaludes. I can't do a little of anything.

My least favorite phrase in the English language is "I don't care." If you ask somebody, "You wanna make love?" or "You wanna play tennis?" and they say, "I don't care" . . . well, fuck you then—I don't want to play.

When I played three-on-three with twenty-year-olds when I was fifty, I didn't care if the guy was six eight—I threw the elbow.

I've never missed a day's work in my life, even through all the shit. But there were days when I was not on my best behavior.

I've been lucky. The critics never went out of their way to single me out for doing bad work.

To get over my divorce, I got a prescription to live at the Playboy Mansion for a while.

I don't think silicone makes a girl good or bad.

People wonder why first-time directors can make a brilliant picture, then suck on the second one. It's because they're a little terrified the first time. So they listen to all the experts around them.

There's nothing more boring than actors talking about acting.

I never saw my dad cry. My son saw me cry. My dad never told me he loved me, and consequently I told Scott I loved him every other minute. The point is, I'll make less mistakes than my dad, my sons hopefully will make less mistakes than me, and their sons will make less mistakes than their dads. And one of these days, maybe we'll raise a perfect Caan.

One day you're playing the boyfriend of Nicole Kidman, the next you're playing her dad. That ain't fun, but whaddya gonna do?

INTERVIEWED BY ROSS JOHNSON // Photograph by Gregg Segal

Robert De Niro

I like it when interviews are brief. Are we done yet?

When I was a teenager, I went to the Dramatic Workshop at the New School. The school had a lot of actors under the GI Bill—Rod Steiger, Harry Belafonte, the generation ahead of me. I went in there and the director said to me, "Vy do you vant to be an acteh?" I didn't know how to answer, so I didn't say anything. And he said, "To express yourself!" And I said, "Yeah, yeah, that's it. That's right."

Some people say, "New York's a great place to visit, but I wouldn't want to live there." I say that about other places.

You have no idea that years later, people in cars will recognize you on the street and shout, "You talkin' to *me*?" I don't remember the original script, but I don't think the line was in it. We improvised. For some reason it touched a nerve. That happens.

Marty Scorsese listens. He's open to unexpected things on that—this is a flowery way of saying it—on that voyage. He takes ideas, and he's not afraid to try them.

There's no such thing as not being afraid.

I left a meeting right after they hit the World Trade Center. I went to my apartment, which looks south, and I watched it out my window. I could see the line of fire across the North Tower. I had my binoculars and a video camera—though I didn't want to video it. I saw a few people jump. Then I saw the South Tower go. It was so unreal, I had to confirm it by immediately looking at the television screen. CNN was on. That was the only way to make it real. Like my son said: "It was like watching the moon fall."

I didn't have a problem with rejection, because when you go into an audition, you're rejected already. There are hundreds of other actors. You're behind the eight ball when you go in there.

At this point in my career, I don't have to deal with audition rejections. So I get my rejection from other things. My children can make me feel rejected. They can humble you pretty quick.

It's true: I spent lunchtime in a grave during the filming of *Bloody Mama*. When you're younger, you feel that's what you need to do to help you stay in character. When you get older, you become more confident and less intense about it—and you can achieve the same effect. You might even be able to achieve more if you take your mind off it, because you're relaxed. That's the key to it all. When you're relaxed and confident, you get good stuff.

The hardest thing about being famous is that people are always nice to you. You're in a conversation and everybody's agreeing with what you're saying—even if you say something totally crazy. You need people who can tell you what you *don't* want to hear.

Movies are hard work. The public doesn't see that. The critics don't see it. But they're a lot of work. A *lot* of work.

When I'm directing a great dramatic scene, part of me is saying, "Thank God I don't have to do that." Because I know how fucking hard it is to act. It's the middle of the night. It's freezing. You gotta do this scene. You gotta get it up to get to that point. And yet, as a director, you've got to get the actors to that point. It's hard either way.

What's the difference between sex and love? Hmm. That's a good question. Hey, you interviewed Al Pacino. How'd *he* answer that?

When a parent dies, it's the end. I always wanted to chronicle the family history with my mother. She was always interested in that. I wanted some researchers I'd worked with to talk to my mother, but my mother was a little antsy about it. I know she would've gotten into it. It would have been okay with my father, too. But I wasn't forceful, and I didn't make it happen. That's one regret I have. I didn't get as much of the family history as I could have for the kids.

As you get older, the more complicated things get. It's almost therapeutic to be doing simple things with the kids.

If you don't go, you'll never know.

INTERVIEWED BY CAL FUSSMAN // Photograph by Sam Jones

bio

BORN: New York, New York
August 17, 1943

> De Niro won Academy Awards for his portrayal of the young Vito Corleone in *The Godfather, Part II* (Best Supporting Actor, 1975) and for his role as boxer Jake La Motta in *Raging Bull* (Best Actor, 1981). He also received an Oscar nomination for *The Deer Hunter* (1978).

> He founded Manhattan's Tribeca Film Center in 1989, which houses his own Tribeca Productions. *A Bronx Tale* (1993) was De Niro's directorial debut.

> In 2002, he organized the first Tribeca Film Festival, now a prominent showcase for filmmakers and part of the economic revitalization of Lower Manhattan.

Kirk Douglas

In order to achieve anything, you must be brave enough to fail.

I tell my sons they didn't have my advantages growing up. I came from abject poverty. There was nowhere to go but up.

Give your children lots of rope. Allow them to make their own mistakes. Don't give them too much advice. Each child is different; you have to respect that. It's a crapshoot: You roll the dice, and you see what happens.

Love has more depth as you get older.

The more I've studied the Torah, the less religious I've become, the more spiritual. We Jews are taught to read Hebrew, but we don't know what the hell we're reading. At Yom Kippur services, I was reading the English translations, and it came to me: There's so much adoration of God, but God doesn't need us to sing his praises. He just wants us to be better people.

Muslims follow Muhammad to reach God. Christians follow Jesus. Jews follow Moses. But it's all the same God.

Everybody has an ego.

I never wanted to be a movie actor. I started out on the stage. The first time I was invited out here, I turned it down. Then Michael was born and I needed money, so I came. Sometimes, the thing that ties you down sets you free.

The learning process continues until the day you die.

If I thought a man had never committed a sin in his life, I don't think I'd want to talk with him. A man with flaws is more interesting.

Making movies is a form of narcissism.

When I kiss my sons on the mouth, people look at me oddly. They look at closeness as a weakness. But a boy needs physical closeness with his father as well as with his mother.

No matter how bad things are, they can always be worse. So what if my stroke left me with a speech impediment? Moses had one, and he did all right.

Mistakes that are perceived as mistakes are often not mistakes at all.

One big disappointment in my life was *One Flew Over the Cuckoo's Nest*. I bought the rights to the book, but no one wanted to make it into a movie. So I paid to have it made into a Broadway play. There was one line in there that was so beautiful. McMurphy is trying to help all these people on the ward. There was a sink, and he tried to lift it out of the wall, but he couldn't. He tried really hard, but it wouldn't budge. As he was leaving the room, with all the guys watching, he turned around and said, "But I tried, goddammit, I tried!" Sometimes I think I should have that as my epitaph.

Politics has become a dirty word.

There must be things in life that you can never master. Golf is one of them.

bio

BORN: Amsterdam, New York
December 9, 1916

> Birth name: Issur Danielovitch Demsky
> Douglas received Academy Award nominations for his performances in *Champion* (1949), *The Bad and the Beautiful* (1952), and *Lust for Life* (1956).
> Other career highlights include *Paths of Glory* (1957), *Spartacus* (1960), and *Posse* (1975), which Douglas directed.
> He has worked as a Goodwill Ambassador for the State Department and the United States Information Agency since 1963, receiving America's highest civilian award, the Presidential Medal of Freedom, in 1981.

Age is in the mind. I've survived a helicopter crash and back surgery. I have a pacemaker. I had a stroke that almost made me commit suicide. But I tell myself, I have to continue growing and functioning. That's the only antidote for age.

Maybe when you die, you come before a big, bearded man on a big throne, and you say, "Is this heaven?" And he says, "Heaven? You just came from there."

Religion has killed millions of people. Something must be wrong.

People are always talking about the old days. They say that the old movies were better, that the old actors were so great. But I don't think so. All I can say about the old days is that they have passed.

I don't like goody-goodies.

The only people who can destroy Israel are the Jews. They are a stiff-necked people, very divisive. It's hard for them all to get along. There's this joke where the president of Israel is talking to the president of America, and he says, "I know it's hard to be the president of a quarter of a billion people, but how would you like to be the president of five million presidents?"

It seems as if only now I really know who I am. My strengths, my weaknesses, my jealousies—it's as if all of it has been boiling in a pot for all these years, and as it boils, it evaporates into steam, and all that's left in the pot in the end is your essence, the stuff you started out with in the very beginning.

INTERVIEWED BY MIKE SAGER // **Photograph by Peggy Sirota**

Faye Dunaway

I'm a bit high maintenance, but it gets your attention. A little hot and cold never hurts.

I regret so much. I've made mistakes. I've hurt people. I've done things I'm not proud of. But on the other hand, that way lies madness, you know?

The impulse toward perfection is more important than perfection itself.

It doesn't really matter what other people think.

Great artists never know if they're making the right choice.

I'm a new Catholic. I love the church; I love mass. I go every morning at 6:30. When I'm on the right track spiritually and emotionally, things happen in my life. It's mysterious.

Hollywood is a hard town to survive.

The thing I love most about men is their sweetness. They're so cute.

Once you reach a certain age, you realize that men aren't as important as you once thought they were.

It's awfully hard to make marriage work. I've tried twice and I don't know how. To have to think of somebody else so much of the time . . . it's such a compromise.

The minute you start believing your own success, you're on the road to ruin.

Fear is a pair of handcuffs on your soul.

The whole era when I was busy being a big movie star was terribly disconcerting. I was cared for and cosseted, and yet I was totally dependent. I didn't know where the cornflakes were kept. I didn't know how to turn on my own washing machine. That might sound very chic, but I'm telling you: When you don't know how your own life works, you get disconnected.

People sell the common man short. Among most people, there is a real impulse toward decency, love, affection, and kindness.

When someone is successful, there's always a feeling that they were lucky. Luck plays a part, sure, but to be successful, you must have iron discipline. You must have energy and hunger and desire and honesty.

Time is enemy number one. Beat time, I say. Kick it!

Without money, there is no freedom. Without money, there is no art. Say what you want, but it's true: When you walk in the door with the money in your hand, people start listening.

The stage might be the only place I really feel at home. I like the greasepaint, the lights, the romance of it all. I like going backstage. I like the ensemble: It's the family that you've always wanted to have; it's like a perfect love, a relationship that is always growing and changing and deepening.

Bonnie Parker was the first role, the one that was closest to me in many ways. She was just this small-town southern girl, coming out of nowhere, hungry and wanting to get ahead, wanting to do something meaningful, wanting to succeed. She had a kind of poetry in her soul. She's a part of me to this day.

The lens is magic. You can love it. It can love you. It captures your innermost feelings and secrets.

Art should predict life.

Sex is emotional. It's connection; it's intimate. It's looking into somebody's soul. It's naked in every sense of the word. It's the hardest thing in the world.

You can't take responsibility for everything. You can't have that kind of control. At some point, it's all out of our hands.

INTERVIEWED BY MIKE SAGER // Photograph by Nigel Parry

bio

BORN: Bascom, Florida
January 14, 1941

> The daughter of a career army officer, Dunaway attended schools in Texas, Arkansas, Utah, and Germany before studying theater at the University of Florida on a Fulbright Scholarship.

> Fame came to Dunaway when she co-starred opposite Warren Beatty in *Bonnie and Clyde* (1967) and appeared in Roman Polanski's *Chinatown* (1974), earning Best Actress nominations for both.

> She finally won an Oscar for her portrayal of television executive Diana Christianson in *Network* (1976).

Jack Nicholson

They're prescription. That's why I wear them. A long time ago, the Middle American in me may have thought it was a bit affected maybe. But the light is very strong in southern California. And once you've experienced negative territory in public life, you begin to accept the notion of shields. I am a person who is trained to look other people in the eye. But I can't look into the eyes of everyone who wants to look into mine; I can't emotionally cope with that kind of volume. Sunglasses are part of my armor.

I hate advice unless I'm giving it.

I hate giving advice, because people won't take it.

I was particularly proud of my performance as the Joker. I considered it a piece of pop art.

The fuel for the sports fan is the ability to have private theories.

I always hesitate to say things like this in interviews because they tend to come back to haunt you, but if I were an Arab-American, I would insist on being profiled. This is not the time for civil rights. There are larger issues for Americans.

My motto is: More good times.

I certainly knew my father. He just didn't happen to be my biological father.

That is correct: I didn't hear that my sister was really my mother until I was thirty-seven years old. But life has taught me that there have been a lot of things that I didn't know. If I start giving what I didn't know more weight because of the half-digested view of an analytical life, it's working against yourself. Accentuate the positive, that's what I say. It's a trick, but it works.

Men dominate because of physicality, and thus they have mercy where women do not.

I respect the social graces enormously. How to pass the food. Don't yell from one room to another. Don't go through a closed door without a knock. Open the doors for the ladies. All these millions of simple household behaviors make for a better life. We can't live in constant rebellion against our parents—it's just silly. I'm very well mannered. It's not an abstract thing. It's a shared language of expectations.

I have to keep myself in check when I go to the kids' sports events. I sit *waaay* in the back. I make sure I don't do too much cheering, you know what I mean? I'm still not quite adjusted to this modern school of thought: Oh, it doesn't matter who wins. I'm not all the way there yet, but I accept it from the back row.

Why can't somebody use modern intelligence and relate it to traffic?

What would it be like to fuck Britney Spears? I can answer that question: monumental. Life altering!

A lot of my life lessons were learned as a child gambler on the boardwalk.

I envy people of faith. I'm incapable of believing in anything supernatural. So far, at least. Not that I wouldn't like to. I mean, I want to believe. I do pray. I pray to something . . . up there. I have a God sense. It's not religious so much as superstitious. It's part of being human, I guess.

Liberalism is the right to question without being called a heretic. That's what America did for the world.

There are major influences on us that people are not aware of. There are big lies that nobody's willing to discuss.

I was influenced in golf by a plaque I read in Kyoto, Japan. It's on a wall of one of the temples. It tells about this Zen archery tournament that had been held there. It's this long colonnade. At the end is a four-inch square. The participants would sit in a cross-legged position, and they'd have to shoot the arrows all the way without hitting the wall. And the world record in the event was something like 180 straight arrows. Knowing sports in the poetic way that I do, this impressed me. So I started thinking of golf as Zen archery.

I get peevish, sure. Nobody yells or screams any more than I do. But the toughest days are when I get home and realize, Holy shit! They were right! Oy, I'm an asshole!

Always try in interviews to avoid the clichés about the problems of public life.

Always try to avoid interviews.

bio

BORN: Neptune, New Jersey
April 22, 1937

> Nicholson rose to stardom in 1969 with the counterculture epic *Easy Rider*, earning an Oscar nomination for Best Supporting Actor.
> He earned another nomination as detective Jake Gittes in Roman Polanski's neo-noir *Chinatown* (1974).
> In 1975, Nicholson starred as McMurphy in Milos Forman's *One Flew Over the Cuckoo's Nest*, the winner of five Oscars including Best Picture and Best Actor. The film earned over $60 million and brought Nicholson enduring fame.
> In addition to his work on screen, Nicholson penned *Head* (1968), a psychedelic saga starring the television pop group the Monkees.

INTERVIEWED BY MIKE SAGER // Photograph by Sam Jones

Al Pacino

My mother died before I made it. You know, here's what I really remember about my mother. We're on the top floor of our tenement. It's freezing out. I have to go to school the next day. I'm maybe ten years old. Down in the alleyway, my friends are calling up to me. They want me to go traveling around with them at night and have some real fun. My mother wouldn't let me. I remember being so angry with her. "Why can't I go out like everyone else? What's wrong with me?" On and on I screamed at her. *She endured my wrath.* And she saved my life. Because those guys down in the alley—none of them are around right now. I don't think about it that much. But it touches me now as I'm talking about it. She didn't want me out in the streets late at night. I had to do my homework. And I'm sitting here right now because of it. It's so simple, isn't it? But we forget, we just forget.

I was a young man when I went to shoot *The Godfather.* I remember being in Sicily, and it was so hot. If you haven't slept and you're not feeling well and it's 120 degrees and you're dressed in all wool, well, you just want to go home. You start feeling, What am I doing? I'm just shooting this over and over again and I don't know what this is anymore. All these Sicilian extras were lined up. They all got wool clothes on, too. This one guy, this Sicilian extra, says in Italian, "We've been out here all day. It's hot. I'd like to take a break." And the production guy says, "You take a break and you're off the picture." Now, the extra obviously has no money, which is why he's doing it in the first place. He looks at the production guy, shrugs his shoulders, says, *"Mah!"* and walks away. And I said to myself, This guy, he's my hero. Could I have done that? No. Could I do it now? *Nahhhhhhhh.* That was freedom.

We were in New York, doing the burial of Don Corleone. We'd shot all day. It's six at night and I'm going home. I see Francis Coppola sitting on the gravestone, and he's crying. Literally bawling. "Francis," I say. "What happened? What's the matter?" And he says, "They won't give me another setup." Meaning, they wouldn't let him shoot the scene again. So he's sitting on the gravestone crying, and I thought, *This guy is going to make a movie here.* If he's got that kind of passion, that kind of feeling about *one* setup . . . That was the moment. I could feel it then. This guy *cares.* And that's it. That's the way to live—around people who *care.* It may be a tough ride, but something is going to come out of it.

One year at the Oscars, I was into whatever altered my mood—a lot of booze, a lot of pills. I've long since stopped. But as I was sitting there during that show, I was thinking, If I get this award, I don't know if I'll be able to get to the stage. That thought paralyzed me. I hope they had the camera on me after Jack Lemmon won, because I was smiling and applauding like the happiest man on the planet.

My father was married five times. What does that tell me? That he liked married life. Okay, what does it *tell* me? It tells me we're creatures of habit.

I've never married. On women, I can be funny and glib. Or I really can try to tell you. Where to start? I have always enjoyed the company of women. I have very close women friends. I could probably sit here for a long time and tell you why that is, or why I think it is. But to say a lot would be an understatement, right?

An actor with too much money will usually find a way to get rid of it.

I like to avoid the word perfection. There's the real apple. And then there's the apple that looks like the perfect apple. The problem is when you bite into the perfect apple, it doesn't have the taste or nourishment of the real apple.

I went to see Frank Sinatra in a concert. This was about twenty years ago. His opening act was Buddy Rich. So Buddy Rich came out, and I wondered about him because Buddy Rich was in his sixties and he was playing the drums. I know he's a good drummer. But I'm thinking, Now I'm going to sit here and listen to him drum for a while and twiddle my thumbs until Frank Sinatra comes out. But once he started and then kept going and going and going, he transcended what I thought he was gonna do tenfold. And it became this *experience.* When Sinatra came out, he said, very simply, "You see this guy drumming? You know, sometimes it's a good idea to stay at a thing."

INTERVIEWED BY CAL FUSSMAN // **Photograph by Platon**

bio

BORN: East Harlem, New York
April 25, 1940

> Pacino dropped out of New York's legendary High School for the Performing Arts at age 17 to pursue his acting career.

> He earned a Best Supporting Actor Oscar nomination for his performance as Michael Corleone in Francis Ford Coppola's epic *The Godfather* (1972).
> Other film highlights include *Dog Day Afternoon* (1975), *Scarface* (1983), *Frankie and Johnny* (1991), *Glengarry Glen Ross* (1992), and *Carlito's Way* (1993).
> Pacino's performance in *Scent of a Woman* (1992) finally landed him an Oscar for Best Actor.

Christopher Reeve

Superman
Bedford, New York

We all have many more abilities and internal resources than we know. My advice is that you don't need to break your neck to find out about them.

Many people at fifty think they've already started to go downhill. I actually think the opposite. I nearly died at forty-two; a neurosurgeon literally had to reconnect my skull to my spinal column. So I survived the accident, survived the surgery, survived ulcers, pneumonia, blood clots, broken bones, and a severe allergic reaction to a drug that almost killed me in July 1995. I've been to the edge much sooner than I ever expected. The fact that I'm still here, gaining rather than losing ground, is very rewarding.

Abe Lincoln put it very simply in 1860: "When I do good, I feel good. When I do bad, I feel bad. That's my religion."

We have a government that, generally speaking, does not respond to the people. Seventy percent of the American public supports embryonic-stem-cell research. And yet it's already been banned by the House and is stalled in the Senate. And we have no federal policy. All the excitement generated in 1998, when embryonic cells were first identified, has pretty much died down. Because scientists don't know what's going to happen in the future. Probably the saddest thing is that most young doctors who would like to go into stem-cell research say, "I can't go into that because this may not be going anywhere for a while, and I've got to pay off my student loans."

Never accept ultimatums, conventional wisdom, or absolutes.

Superman is a big fish in a small pond. He's Superman on Earth only because he's in a different solar system. If he'd grown up on Krypton, if Krypton had not been destroyed, he might have been average—nothing special about him. That allowed me to underplay the character and make him quite casual.

Some people are walking around with full use of their bodies and they're more paralyzed than I am.

In the first few years after the accident, people were almost *too* respectful. I remember going on *Letterman*. He was so serious, almost reverential, that I had to crack jokes to keep the interview alive. But over the years, that's virtually disappeared because people see that I'm living a full and active life. Now it's almost the other way around. What happened to the pity?

In rehab, I saw both extremes: Good relationships grew stronger, and ones that were in trouble fell apart.

I used to say to my wife, Dana, all the time, "I really put the marriage vows to the test. This is not what we meant by 'in sickness and in health.' "

You get used to the need to be taken care of in the bathroom.

I'm often accused of being too aggressive with researchers, saying, "Why can't you go faster? Why can't you get to the human trials sooner? Please appreciate the fact that the patient population is willing to accept reasonable risks."

It's been relatively easy to get the support of politicians who have an emotional connection to disease and disability. For example, Senator Harkin has a nephew with a spinal-cord injury. Now you see Nancy Reagan working behind the scenes, lobbying for stem-cell research beyond the limitations imposed by Bush in August 2001, and you think back to the early '80s, when she and her husband were in office and opposed federal funding for AIDS research. Thousands of people died. It's helpful that she's asking senators to back therapeutic cloning to create more stem-cell lines. But the way I see it, she's doing it now only because Ronnie doesn't recognize her. Why do people wait until it hurts?

To really become free inside takes either courage or disaster. Certainly to my kids I recommend courage.

If you came back here in ten years, I expect that I'd walk to the door to greet you.

bio

BORN: New York, New York
September 25, 1952

> Best-known for his starring role in *Superman: The Movie* (1978), Reeve beat out Robert Redford, Sylvester Stallone, and Clint Eastwood for the job.
> Reeve's performance as the Man of Steel only served to intensify the tragedy of his June 1995 accident, when he fell from a horse during a steeplechase race. The accident broke several key bones in his neck and left him completely paralyzed.
> In 1996, Reeve helped establish the UCI Reeve-Irvine Research Center, which specializes in spinal cord injuries. He also opened the Christopher and Dana Reeve Paralysis Center, a facility in Short Hills, New Jersey, devoted to teaching paralyzed people to live more independently.

INTERVIEWED BY CAL FUSSMAN // Photograph by Chris Floyd

Rod Steiger

Actor
Malibu, California

Fantasies of success should never precede endeavor.

Only those who give you the best can give you the worst.

Thought is like a snowball: The longer you live, the more it melts.

Fear is an impossible thing to avoid.

Pain is a teacher that must be understood.

There is a need for tears at the beginning of sorrow; that's the instant release. But to cry and not to gain is complete defeat. You must control the force of terror so it begins to work for you.

Nothing should be worshiped except accomplishments and courage.

False hope is unnecessary pain.

Time is the pawnbroker of values.

He who hesitates is bossed.

Man is cursed with the ambition to be the best hunter in the tribe. When a guy came home to the village covered with blood, there was no argument when he asked for a gourd of water or a piece of ass.

When a guy came home to the village covered with blood, there was no argument when he asked for a gourd of water or a piece of ass.

Do not make the mistake of trying to revisit a memory.

Curiosity will lead you to many little deaths and many little happinesses.

The day your curiosity dies, your life is over.

What you don't know will scare the shit out of you.

Respecting differences is very difficult.

To be desired puts you in command. It can be an incredible gift or a malignant weapon.

Success means controlling your own time. If you can gain control over 60 percent of the time in your life, you are really successful. Time is the most important currency, but once you spend it, man, it is gone.

True freedom can't exist without emotional satisfaction.

Freedom without responsibility is chaos.

In the fifties, I went to see this analyst. It was the vogue. I told him, "Now, look, before we go into this—I have to be free to create; I have to be free to do things. I have to be free to get up when I want, sleep with anyone I want, do what I want to do. I can't be regimented; I have to be free!" And he said, "That's fine. Just be careful you don't become a slave to freedom."

You're not supposed to understand everything.

Surprise is the lubrication of adventure.

Too much pleasure, you're destroyed; too much nonpleasure, you're destroyed.

The greatest pleasures in the world are exciting, harmless secrets we don't tell anyone.

If I could find a way to have sex with myself that was as exciting as it is with a lady, I'd live in a white tower and never come out.

We get confused between self-esteem and narcissism.

A so-called deficit in your childhood can be an asset as you get older.

Anything I ever learned comes down to something pretty simple: Don't anticipate life; meet it. When you try to anticipate, you're being an idiot, because nobody's got the brain to outwit nature. I'm talking here about patience, about believing in yourself. I'm talking here about having the courage to wait. You will get what you deserve.

INTERVIEWED BY MIKE SAGER // Photograph by Dan Winters

bio

BORN: Westhampton, New York
April 14, 1925
DIED: Los Angeles, California, July 9, 2002

> Steiger appeared in over 100 films including *On the Waterfront* (1954), *The Pawnbroker* (1965), and *The Hurricane* (1999). He won an Oscar for his role opposite Sidney Poitier in *In the Heat of the Night* (1967).
> He turned down lead roles in *Patton* (1970) and *The Godfather* (1972).
> Steiger's prolific career makes him the most linkable actor in the Internet Movie Database. The average "degrees of separation" of a film actor from Steiger is 2.660 (compared to Kevin Bacon's 2.943).

Rip Torn

I've never hit anybody who hasn't clocked me two or three times.

Everybody says, You impress me as a guy who never wanted to be a movie star. I say, Everybody in the world wants to be a movie star.

I don't give my children advice unless they ask. If I have a few things, I try to boil it down to a telegram.

I washed dishes at Bob's, the Home of the Big Boy, Glendale, California. I went in there to get that job, and the guy says, "You're not an actor, are ya?" I says, "Hell, no." It was the first outfit to have photographs of the food on its menu. The guy says, "That was my idea." I says, "And the waitresses are so beautiful." He says, "Yes, I pick them." I says, "This is the job for me."

The famous saying about reviews is, If you believe the good ones, you'll believe the bad ones. It's better to look at 'em after you've finished the run.

When people used to say, I hear you're a Method actor, I'd say, Wrong. I'm a Methodist actor.

When I drove my son around to show him where I had fished with my grandfather, some of the richest land in Texas, a big condo had been built where I used to fish. I started laughing. Then I was crying at the same time. The relentless onslaught of overdevelopment. I don't think it makes you a radical to oppose that. It makes you a conservative.

I said to my dad, "I don't know why I feel so much at home here in Times Square. I feel a kinship here the same way I do about Texas." He said, "That's easy to understand." I said, "How so?" He said, "Well"—we looked up and we were on Seventh Avenue and Fiftieth Street—"you were conceived on the top floor of the Taft Hotel." I said, "Are you sure?" He said, "As sure as any man could ever be." Maybe it's like some of the fish, steelhead, that come back to the place where they started life.

bio

BORN: Temple, Texas
February 6, 1931

> Birth name: Elmore Rual Torn. His father gave him the nickname.
> Torn made a name for himself on television in the late fifties, appearing on such prestigious live shows as *Omnibus*, *Playhouse 90*, and *Alfred Hitchcock Presents*.
> He played Larry Sanders's producer on the acclaimed cable sitcom *The Larry Sanders Show* (1992 to 1998). For this work, he won a pair of Cable Ace Awards, three Emmy nominations, and one Emmy for Best Supporting Actor in a comedy series.

When I grew up, people said, You'll never be the man your dad was. And I said, Gee, I hope not.

I used to be friends with Miles Davis. He didn't like many folks. I lived across the street from him. He would call me up sometimes—"I got some fish I wanna cook up for ya." I went up there, and he was on a couch, looking out the window. He was just rapt. I said, "What're you watching, Miles?" He said, "The traffic. Where are all these motherfuckers goin'?"

They don't have Polish jokes in Texas. They have Aggie jokes.

Be your own politics, grow your own garden, and maybe you can help out more.

I think most actors are shy. I really do. The greatest actors can disappear. I had friends call me the Blend-In Man.

If you're lucky enough to have a pretty girl love you and share herself and sleep with you, make that your secret. The best way to spoil love is by talking to too many people about it.

I asked Laurence Olivier what was the key to acting. He said, "Physical strength."

Never think you're better than anyone else, but don't let anyone treat you like you're worse than they are.

A lot of times, tough-guy types will see me and say, Oh, man, I always thought you were a great big guy; you're just a squirt. I just say, Don't make a mistake.

You can never turn your back on the ocean.

When I get to Texas, I generally go and get some good brisket. And I'll get a selection of cabrito and lamb and some hot sausage. And a big slice of onion. And I'll sit down and have a good beer. Shiner.

Don't ever humiliate a man. If you're gonna have to dress him out, you take him aside and do it that way. That's the one thing I don't like about Hollywood: They go in for public humiliation. You shouldn't do that to a man.

There's always some kind of blacklist throughout history. But the difference is, in America they usually let you live.

Garry Shandling always said to me, "Don't get mad, get funny." It changed my life.

Let the other guys do the crybaby stuff. Go for the laughs.

If you read Shakespeare, you realize it was ever thus.

INTERVIEWED BY SCOTT RAAB // Photograph by Nigel Parry

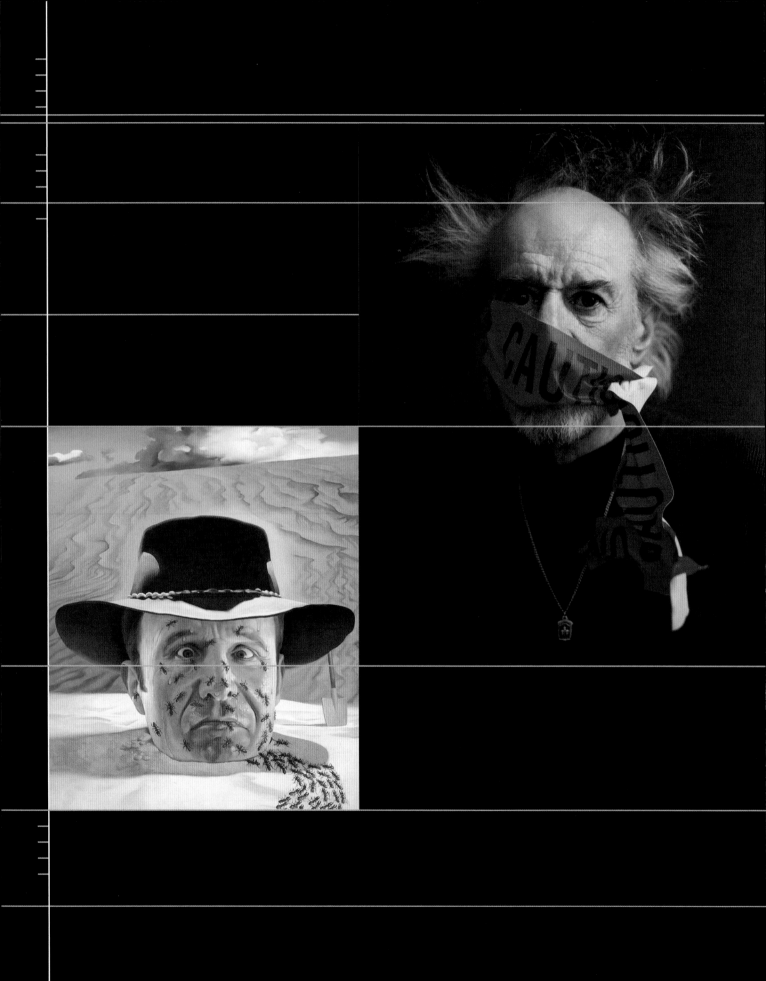

The Trailblazers

Mark Burnett

George Carlin

Julia Child

Hugh Hefner

Charles H. Townes

Mark Burnett

Television producer
Santa Monica, California

In television, nobody really knows anything.

Bug eating and backstabbing are the stuff of great entertainment.

If you believe in something, go with it. Rarely listen to others.

If you have some success, you'll find many new friends.

The anticipation of a problem is far worse than the problem itself.

Americans are very giving. They're very pro-risk. They're interested in results—not what you tell them or which school you went to or who you know. America equals meritocracy. I'm all for it.

You must learn to have confidence when you're only half sure. If you need to be 100 percent sure, that's called procrastination.

You couldn't have sixteen Richard Hatches. It wouldn't work.

All human beings have good intentions. We tell ourselves we're not going to say a certain thing to a loved one, that we're not going to do a certain thing at work. But we always fall back into the same patterns. We're all just who we are.

Deprivation causes deeper relationships.

God is the first name used when things go wrong.

The more comfortable our society becomes, the more we seek adventure. If you look at the demographics, the number of backpacks, tents, and mountain bikes being sold is at an all-time high. It's because we're looking for something deeper. You're not going to find the meaning of life sitting at your desk with your thumb up your ass and your brain in neutral. You're only going to find the meaning of life with a little bit of pain, in the outdoors, where nature is in command and you feel vulnerable and you start to feel a little bit scared. That's when you find out who you really are.

Everybody's out for themselves. We may be charitable at times, but very few are out for others. Maybe Mother Teresa.

Religion is a waste of time. I can't understand how millions of Muslims could be wrong. Or millions of Jews. Or millions of Hindus. How can they all be wrong and only one religion be right?

You can't take yourself too seriously. Like Rudyard Kipling said, You have to learn to treat success and failure as impostors, just the same.

If you're as selfish as I am, marriage is very difficult.

Fear is the greatest motivator.

Survivor is based on real life. We've all met people like this. We've all experienced workplace politics. We've all dealt with these situations—people befriending you, people stabbing you in the back. It's duplicity and hardball. It's serious emotions. We can identify.

The wilderness is the only place I want to be.

It's hard to trust anybody.

Most people are waiting around for someone to lead.

In sales, you better know your product. You better be confident. You better be inspiring. And you better be able to deliver.

The most important element to survival is adaptability, the ability to change your goals and needs. The second-most important element to survival is a positive outlook; once something's gone wrong, the only thing left to do is to deal with it.

I've known hardship. I don't really want it anymore.

Survivor is as much a marketing vehicle as it is a television show. My shows create an interest, and people will look at them, but the endgame here is selling products in stores—a car, deodorant, running shoes. It's the future of television.

Obviously I believe in God. Look at me right now.

INTERVIEWED BY MIKE SAGER // Illustration by Roberto Parada

bio

BORN: London, England
July 17, 1960

> Executive producer of CBS's groundbreaking reality television show, *Survivor*. Burnett went on to make *The Restaurant* and *The Apprentice*, co-produced with Donald Trump.

> He came to America at age 22, and the only job he could find was a temporary gig as a live-in nanny in Beverly Hills. He held several other nanny and babysitting jobs after that, and also worked as a T-shirt vendor in Venice Beach.

> Burnett loves to scuba dive and jump out of planes. He has completed a white water guide course and is certified in advanced wilderness first aid.

George Carlin

Comedian
Venice, California

I was in my mother's belly as she sat in the waiting room of the abortionist's office. Dr. Sunshine was his code name. I was fifty feet from the drainpipe, and she saw a painting on the wall that reminded her of her mother, who had recently died. She took that as a sign to have the baby. That's what I call luck.

My father drank and was a bully. For the first five years of my brother's life, my father beat him with a leather-heeled slipper. Had I been subjected to that kind of treatment, all bets are off. His absence saved my life.

My mother had great executive-secretarial jobs in the advertising business and raised two boys during the Second World War. She used to say, "I make a man's salary." That's heroism.

I'm sure Hitler was great with his family.

I used to collect the most colorful curses I heard and write them down. I actually carried in my wallet things like "kraut cunt" and "burly loudmouth cocksucker" and "longhair fucking music prick," which was a thing Mikey Flynn yelled at a Juilliard student that he was kicking in the head.

Sex without love has its place, and it's pretty cool, but when you have it hand in hand with deep commitment and respect and caring, it's nine thousand times better.

If it's morally wrong to kill anyone, then it's morally wrong to kill anyone. Period.

It's amazing to me that literacy isn't considered a right.

BORN: Bronx, New York
May 12, 1937

> In the late 1960s, Carlin's landmark routine, "Seven Words You Can Never Say on Television," explored the limits of free speech and good taste.
> In 1975, he was the first guest-host of NBC's *Saturday Night Live.* In 1988, he re-emerged to appeal to a new generation as a star of *Bill and Ted's Excellent Adventure.*
> Carlin's 18 comedy albums have earned numerous Grammy nominations and awards. He has also earned five Emmy nominations and six CableAce Awards.

I was arrested for possession and cultivation of marijuana in the early '70s, and it was thrown out. The judge asked me how I felt about it, and I said, "I understand the law, and I want you to know I'll pay the fine, but I cannot guarantee I will not break this law again." He really chewed me out for that.

Censorship that comes from the outside assumes about people an inability to make reasoned choices.

The first thing they teach kids is that there's a God—an invisible man in the sky who is watching what they do and who is displeased with some of it. There's no mystery why they start that with kids, because if you can get someone to believe that, you can add on anything you want.

I wish that we could measure how much the potential of the mind to expand has been stunted by television.

Because of my abuse of drugs, I neglected my business affairs and had large arrears with the IRS, and that took me eighteen to twenty years to dig out of. I did it honorably, and I don't begrudge them. I don't hate paying taxes, and I'm not angry at anyone, because I was complicit in it. But I'll tell you what it did for me: It made me a way better comedian. Because I had to stay out on the road and I couldn't pursue that movie career, which would have gone nowhere, and I became a really good comic and a really good writer.

I stopped voting when I stopped taking drugs. I believe both of those acts are closely related to delusional behavior.

There's no morality in business. It doesn't have a conscience. It has only the cash register. They'll sell you crappy things that you don't need, that don't work, that they won't stand behind. It's a glorified legal form of criminal behavior.

There's nothing wrong with high taxes on high income.

Lenny Bruce opened all the doors, and people like Richard Pryor and I were able to walk through them.

Given the right reasons and the right two people, marriage is a wonderful way of experiencing your life.

I think that the assassinations of the Kennedys and Martin Luther King showed that all of the wishing and hoping and holding hands and humming and signing petitions and licking envelopes is a bit futile.

I don't think people should get credit for being honest and brave. I think there's a lot of genetic shit going on there.

If there's ever a golden age of mankind, it will not include men over two hundred pounds beating children who are less than one hundred pounds, and it will not include the deliberate killing of people in a formal setting.

I did something in a previous life that must have been spectacularly good, because I'm getting paid in this life just magnificently, more than one would dare imagine or hope for.

INTERVIEWED BY LARRY GETLEN // Photograph by Peggy Sirota

Julia Child

Fat gives things flavor.

People are uncertain because they don't have the self-confidence to make decisions.

The measure of achievement is not winning awards. It's doing something that you appreciate, something you believe is worthwhile. I think of my strawberry soufflé. I did that at least twenty-eight times before I finally conquered it.

Playing golf with men can throw off your stroke.

Being tall is an advantage, especially in business. People will always remember you. And if you're in a crowd, you'll always have some clean air to breathe.

There is nothing worse than grilled vegetables.

Celebrity has its uses: I can always get a seat in any restaurant.

I was faced by my nieces and good friends and told I shouldn't drive my car anymore. Actually, I find I'm not quite as alert as I used to be, and it would be awful to kill somebody. So now I don't drive, and it is real hell, because you can't rush down to the store and get a bunch of parsley if you have the whim, or do something like that. It's just awful not driving, because you have to depend on other people. You get used to it, though. They have a bus here—I haven't tried it yet, but I shall.

A cookbook is only as good as its poorest recipe.

I hate organized religion. I think you have to love thy neighbor as thyself. I think you have to pick your own God and be true to him. I always say "him" rather than "her." Maybe it's because of my generation, but I don't like the idea of a female God. I see God as a benevolent male.

I'm awfully sorry for people who are taken in by all of today's dietary mumbo jumbo. They are not getting any enjoyment out of their food.

Moderation. Small helpings. Sample a little bit of everything. These are the secrets of happiness and good health. You need to enjoy the good things in life, but you need not overindulge.

I went into a doctor's office the other day and all the people—you know, the nurses and the receptionists and even the patients—were sort of short-tempered and not very nice. And it made me think, I just want to bop them over the head. It's terribly important to keep a good temper.

I don't eat between meals. I don't snack. Well, I do eat those little fish crackers. They're fattening, but irresistible.

The problem with the world right now is that we don't have any politicians like Roosevelt or Churchill to give us meaning and depth. We don't have anyone who's speaking for the great and the true and the noble. What we need now is a heroic type, someone who could rally the people to higher deeds. I don't know what's to become of us.

You must have discipline to have fun.

Drama is very important in life: You have to come on with a bang. You never want to go out with a whimper. Everything can have drama if it's done right. Even a pancake.

I don't believe in heaven. I think when we die we just go back to the great ball of energy that makes up the universe.

Hell only exists on earth, when you've made mistakes and you're paying for them.

I don't think about whether people will remember me or not. I've been an okay person. I've learned a lot. I've taught people a thing or two. That's what's important. Sooner or later the public will forget you, the memory of you will fade. What's important are the individuals you've influenced along the way.

Always remember: If you're alone in the kitchen and you drop the lamb, you can always just pick it up. Who's going to know?

INTERVIEWED BY MIKE SAGER // Illustration by Roberto Parada

bio

BORN: Pasadena, California
August 15, 1912

> Born: Julia McWilliams. A graduate of the prestigious women's school Smith College (1934), Child was the only woman in her class at Le Cordon Bleu in Paris.
> *The French Chef*, Child's long-running PBS television series,

is credited with introducing American audiences to French cuisine. The program is now syndicated on the Food Network.
> Her first cookbook, *Mastering the Art of French Cooking* (1961), is still widely available. She's published dozens of other cookbooks including *Julia and Jacques: Cooking at Home with Jacques Pepin* (1999).
> Child's television kitchen, with its extra-high counters to accommodate her six-foot-plus frame, has been preserved by the Smithsonian.

Hugh Hefner

If they say Hef, they know me. If they say Hugh, they don't.

I have slept with thousands of women, and they all still like me.

Women were the major beneficiary of the sexual revolution. It permitted them to be natural sexual beings, as men are. That's where feminism should have been all along. Unfortunately, within feminism, there has been a puritan, prohibitionist element that is antisexual.

Playboy is the antidote to puritanism.

In the 1950s and '60s, there were still states that outlawed birth control, so I started funding court cases to challenge that. At the same time, I helped sponsor the lower-court cases that eventually led to *Roe* v. *Wade*. We were the *amicus curiae* in *Roe* v. *Wade*. I was a feminist before there was such a thing as feminism. That's a part of history very few people know.

Sex is *the* driving force on the planet. We should embrace it, not see it as the enemy.

There isn't a whole lot of point to living half the year in a lousy climate.

Every man should have a Hitachi Wand. It's a very good vibrator.

We're separated by our myths.

One of the problems with organized religion is that it has always kept women in a second-class position. They have been viewed as the daughters of Eve.

I stand in total awe of existence. I don't pretend to know what it's about.

My best pick-up line is "My name is Hugh Hefner."

Most people don't have much of a clue as to why they act the way they do. Usually when they're angry, they're not angry about what they think they're angry about.

It's good to be selfish. But not so self-centered that you never listen to other people.

Hollywood has many, many excesses and a great many not very nice people, but that's true anywhere. The difference between Hollywood and New York is that it's all out in the open.

Living in the moment, thinking about the future, and staying connected to the past: That's what makes me feel whole.

A lot of people go through life never quite understanding that if things aren't as wonderful as they should be, it's their own fault.

When I'm alone, masturbation isn't bad. But I don't spend a lot of time alone.

There's a real hypocrisy about people who pursue fame for the first half of their lives and then pretend to resent it afterward.

What surprises me about getting older is that I remain so young.

If you don't have a sense of humor about life and yourself, then you are old.

Gloria Steinem said that a woman needs a man like a fish needs a bicycle. And now she's married to a wealthy guy. So what does that say to you?

Everybody, if they've got their head on straight, wants to be a sexual object, among other things. They want to be attractive. Otherwise, what a sad and pathetic life. To really live a worthwhile life is to be attracted to and attractive to other people.

One of the great ironies in our society is that we celebrate freedom and then limit the parts of life where we should be most free.

When you are in a position to not be a nice person, that's when you find out who you really are.

I wake up every day and go to bed every night knowing I'm the luckiest guy on the fucking planet.

My house is pretty much in order. When it comes, it comes. But my mother lived to be 101, so knock on wood.

My favorite nightcap is Jack Daniel's and Coke. Or Pepsi. You get the Jack Daniel's in there, it doesn't matter.

My views have evolved from childhood, but I haven't changed my mind in a very dramatic way. I've always felt I was on the side of the angels.

My life is an open book. With illustrations.

INTERVIEWED BY WIL S. HYLTON // **Photograph by Peggy Sirota**

bio

BORN: Chicago, Illinois
April 9, 1926

> Hefner was working in *Esquire's* promotion department when he left to found *Playboy*.
> When *Playboy* hit newsstands in December 1953, the magazine carried no cover date because Hefner was not sure when or if he would be able to produce another issue. But the first one sold more than 50,000 copies and he was in business.
> The magazine originally posed a challenge to the U.S. Post Office and its anti-obscenity regulations. No one had ever attempted to establish a mainstream commercial venture by sending nude pictures through the mail.
> When Playboy Enterprises went public in 1971, it sold seven million copies of the magazine in one month.

Charles H. Townes

Science is exploration. The fundamental nature of exploration is that we don't know what's there. We can guess and hope and aim to find out certain things, but we have to expect surprises. Look at Columbus: He was aiming for India. Well, he missed it. He found something else.

Listen to other people, but don't necessarily follow them.

God is very difficult to define, but I feel his presence. I feel an omnipresence everywhere and something, at the same time, rather personal. In religion, people talk about revelations. In science you find many revelations, too, it's just that people don't talk about them that way. When the idea for the laser came to me, I was sitting on a park bench thinking, Now, why haven't I been able to do this? Suddenly a new idea comes to me, a new creation. Where did it come from? Did God give me this idea? Who knows? I didn't suddenly have a view of God's face, if that's what you mean. In science we just don't talk about it much. You say, Well, I had an *idea*. In the religious world people talk about revelations. They are not so basically different.

I realized there would be many applications for the laser, but it never occurred to me we'd get such power from it. Recently people made a laser beam of a million billion watts. That's more power than is used on earth at any one time.

Why does time always move in one direction? That's strange. If we move forward, we can also move backward; if we move up, we can also move down. Time is like a dimension of space in many ways, and yet we can't go backward.

With the big bang, there is a unique moment in the past. Now, one can ask, What was before *that*? You can say God created the universe, but who created God? So there's always a problem with a beginning.

What makes a marriage work? Genuineness of commitment and devotion. One has to be able to forgive.

If you think of intelligence as knowing a lot of things, of responding quickly and brightly, you can recognize that. But if you think of intelligence as someone who is creative, someone who can think new things and think deeper thoughts, that's not always easy to recognize. People have different characteristics.

Change fields every one or two decades. Some people stay in one field all their life and develop it more and more and more, and that's useful. I myself think it is more fun to explore new things.

We can't avoid age. However, we can avoid some aging. Continue to do things. Be active. Life is fantastic in the way it adjusts to demands; if you use your muscles and mind, they stay there much longer.

In many cases, people who win a Nobel Prize, their work slows down after that because of the distractions. Yes, fame is rewarding, but it's a pity if it keeps you from doing the work you are good at.

It's not technology itself that's bad, it's what we do with it.

Zero is a useful concept. So is infinity.

The laws of physics are very special, and the creation of human life is really quite striking. One has to believe that either it was planned or it was a fantastically improbable accident.

The reality of the afterlife one can debate. But whatever you do in life affects other people, and that remains.

There are lots of very powerful, naturally occurring water masers in interstellar space.

I feel that very rarely have I done any work in my life. I have a good time. I'm exploring. I'm playing a game, solving puzzles, and having fun, and for some reason people have been willing to pay me for it. Officially, I was supposed to retire years ago, but retire from what? Why stop having a good time?

Some people would say that because we don't know, it can't be. I would say that because we don't know, we don't know.

INTERVIEWED BY SCOTT CARRIER // Photograph by Dan Winters

bio

BORN: Greenville, South Carolina
July 28, 1915

> Dr. Townes has been a professor of physics at Columbia University, MIT, and, most recently, the University of California at Berkeley.

> As a member of the technical staff of Bell Telephone Laboratories, he designed radar bombing systems during World War II.
> He shared the Nobel Prize in physics in 1964, receiving one-half of a three-way prize. (The other two scientists, Nicolay G. Basov and Alexsander M. Prokhorov, each received one-quarter of the credit.)

The
Voices

Ray Charles

Elvis Costello

Al Green

Loretta Lynn

Willie Nelson

Elvis Presley

Lou Reed

Lucinda Williams

Ray Charles

Musician
Los Angeles

Music is about the only thing left that people don't fight over.

People couldn't understand why my mama would have this blind kid out doing things like cutting wood for the fire. But her thing was: He may be blind, but he ain't stupid.

I remember one night we did a thing with Duke Ellington. He was on an oxygen tank until they called him to come out onstage. But he went out there and you'd never have known there was anything wrong with the man. That's what music can do. If you're sad, you can go home and play some records and make yourself feel better. If you're in the hospital and you're sick, music can be soothing. I know I'm gonna get shot down for this, but I think music is the greatest art form ever, bar none. I know that people who are into movies or into sculpture or writing or whatever are gonna say, "Ray, you must done lost your brain." And they probably right. But I still think that music is the greatest art form ever.

They say war has a purpose, but I'm not sure I agree.

I've always thought that people want you to be one of two things: They either want you to be a clone—meaning just like them—or they want you to be their footstool, so they can control you and tell you what to do.

Sighted people sometimes forget that blind people have a mind.

I don't analyze myself. I just do what I do.

You better live every day like it's your last day, 'cause one day you're gonna be right.

I'm a firm believer in God himself, but that's as far as I can go. I'm not any denomination. I'm not Catholic or Presbyterian or Baptist or Methodist or Jewish or Muslim. I'm none of those things. And I'm sure that's just fine with God.

I did drugs because it was my pleasure.

The piano is the foundation, and that's it.

All my kids know me.

Addiction can be very, very bad. But addiction in itself isn't bad; it's a question of what you're addicted to. That's where the chickens come home to roost. You can be addicted to good habits, you know what I mean? You can be addicted to your woman. Addiction in itself is kind of like money. It ain't bad or good. It's what you do with it.

When you write a good song, it will be good even if it's sung by somebody with a bad voice.

We always gonna have racism.

With singing, the name of the game is to make yourself believable. When somebody hears you sing a song and they say, "Oh, that must have happened to him," that's when you know you're transmitting. It's like being a good actor. You make people feel things, emotions and whatnot. But you gotta start with yourself. You got to feel it yourself. If you don't feel it, how do you expect someone else to?

I don't remember much about what it was like to see. The main thing I remember is my mom, how she looked.

People say: "Ray, you a genius, Ray, you a cornerstone, Ray, you this and you that." Those are nice accolades, and I certainly appreciate it when people think well of my music and what I've tried to do with it. But in my heart, I mean . . . I don't kid myself. I know I'm not a genius. A genius is somebody like Art Tatum or Charlie Parker. I don't come close to those guys. I just happen to be a guy that can do a lot of little things and do 'em well.

It would be a real bitch if I ever lost my hearing. I know I couldn't be no Helen Keller. That would be worse than death.

Vision is something that you have in your mind.

This is a girl's bike, man. Why would I be riding a girl's bike? You didn't think I was gonna notice that, right? You guys are trying to sucker a blind man!

INTERVIEWED BY MIKE SAGER // Photograph by Gregg Segal

bio

BORN: Albany, Georgia
September 23, 1930

> Although he was blinded by glaucoma at the age of six, Charles learned to read and write music and could play several musical instruments by the time he left school.
> His music career took off in the '50s with singles such as "It Should Have Been Me," "I Got a Woman," and "What'd I Say."
> One of the first artists to marry gospel and R & B, Charles has performed blues, jazz, and country, stamping his own style on everything he plays.
> He has 12 Grammys and was inducted into the Rock and Roll Hall of Fame in 1986.
> A long-time advocate of racial justice, Charles befriended Martin Luther King in the '60s. He also supported the fight against apartheid in South Africa, among other humanitarian efforts.

Elvis Costello

Songwriter
Dublin

What have I learned? Well, you can answer that on so many levels, can't you? You can answer it on a philosophical level, or you can say, "I know this restaurant," or "Always get the foam pillow."

I was in a room with Chuck Berry once. I said to myself, I don't want to meet you. I just want to look at you. He was scary.

We're all just animals. That's all we are, and everything else is just an elaborate justification of our instincts. That's where music comes from. And romantic poetry. And bad novels. Sometimes when I finish a bad novel, I say, "You wrote seven hundred pages just to say *that*? Couldn't you have just said, 'I want to fuck'?"

Fruit helps in the middle of the day.

Happiness isn't a fortune in a cookie. It's deeper, wider, funnier, and more transporting than that.

I'm not very good at joyful.

You need to meet Sting. He's a totally charming guy. He's always been a nice guy, very good-looking, he's got a good voice—it's not a voice I like particularly, but he's written one or two really beautiful songs, and he's been extraordinarily fortunate in many ways. He's some people's idea of sophisticated. He plays the corporate events; maybe nobody invites him to any better parties. But there's always somebody in music who's equivalent to that role, and I think he's easy to hold up as kind of an Aunt Sally.

BORN: Liverpool, England
August 25, 1954

> Birth name: Declan Patrick MacManus. "Elvis" was a challenge to the rock establishment, and "Costello" was his mother's maiden name.
> When Costello's first two singles failed to gain attention, he strapped an amplifier to his back and played in the street outside a CBS Records convention in London. Costello was arrested, but signed with the label nonetheless.
> His first album, *My Aim Is True* (1977), was embraced by the new wave and underground punk scene and voted *Rolling Stone*'s Album of the Year.
> He married the jazz singer Diana Krall on December 6, 2003.

I don't think he's an insincere musician. He just doesn't seem to value the same things about music that I do.

Songs are more powerful than books.

Elvis probably had a little more curiosity than the next kid, and that's why he was him.

In John Lennon's songs, people tend to isolate the lines that sound like epitaphs or greeting cards. It's very odd to drive by the Liverpool airport and see the logo with his drawing and the words "Above us only sky." The sky is full of planes! But everybody becomes a mass-pattern tablecloth in the end.

I've seen a lot of exotic places in my work and all my traveling. But the place I still want to see is the place in somebody's eyes. You know: Travel less, see more.

I don't like that idea, eye surgery. I won't be getting that. It's like penile enlargement or something.

Living a very long time would be a very scary thing.

Eventually we'll need jet packs to get around and space helmets with Ventolin in them to allow us to breathe. Do you know what Ventolin is? It's what asthmatics take. A lot of kids have asthma now. We've done a good job at mucking things up.

Read the magazines at the margins of the music industry. That's where most of the interesting music is.

They used to just get on with things, didn't they? They had the blues then. They understood the idea of the blues.

I used to wear these blue lenses all the time. You really do get depressed if you wear blue lenses. When people say, "You're looking at the world through rose-colored glasses," well, I have no idea what rose ones do, but I know what blue ones do. They make you sad.

I didn't even own a Bob Dylan record until 1971. To me, he was a great singles artist. You heard him on the radio. What a shocking thing to live in a world where there was Manfred Mann and the Supremes and Engelbert Humperdinck and here comes "Like a Rolling Stone." That was a great world, a very exciting time.

The assumption that something is not for you is an assumption that can be undone in time.

It's very important to allow yourself the ability to have a second thought. Because if you put everything into breaking down the door, what are you going to say when you get in there?

Singing with Emmylou Harris: If there is heaven, that's what it's like.

People don't know that music can affect your sense of smell, but it can.

All songs are motivated by revenge or guilt? Did I say that? I must have been full of Pernod.

There are about five things to write songs about: I'm leaving you. You're leaving me. I want you. You don't want me. I believe in something. Five subjects, and twelve notes. For all that, we musicians do pretty well.

INTERVIEWED BY TOM JUNOD // **Photograph by Mark Seliger**

Al Green

A prostitute is a poor thing to put confidence in.

There was ten of us, five boys and five girls, and Mom and Dad made twelve people in one house, a little two-bedroom. Daddy couldn't buy everybody shoes at one time, so somebody's getting hand-me-downs. That's me.

I didn't have a mother; I had a mama. I measure other women by the stature of my mama.

Daddy used to go to the honky-tonk bars and leave me in the truck. After a while, he'd come out staggering and slurring, "Now, don't you tell your mama what I did, boy." He was so drunk, I wouldn't have to say anything.

Everything is handed to society now. Before, you had to dig for it. I like that—digging for it.

What if she takes your heart and wraps it around her little finger and has you going to the store, shopping, washing clothes, and then she breaks your heart? That's the chance you've got to take on love.

I was a fantastic womanizer. I mean, I was incredible. I just didn't know what I was doing. I had women all over the place, they were all over me, and my dad said, "Well, why don't you just choose one?"

I don't know what bad music is if it's done right, but then again, I don't know what good music is if it's done wrong.

A man's gift makes room for him.

Blacks have based their feelings on "What happened to me, being a slave on the plantation, da da da," and that's fine and dandy. But I could go to my friend Henry, who's Jewish, and say, "What happened to you?" And he'd say, "My grandparents died in the Holocaust." So that stuff happened to everybody.

Look at you. The chains you had on. Now they're gold.

You can't sleep all day and get up at 4:00 in the evening and pretend you're in a hurry.

The trick to achieving a good falsetto? I know no way to accomplish that. I don't even know how I sing like I sing.

Church is so important for black people because it's the only place we had to go when we couldn't go no place else. Couldn't go to the bar—wasn't allowed. Couldn't go to the hotel because we weren't able to rent a room. Couldn't go to the restaurant because we weren't allowed to be seated. So we went to church.

If there wasn't a hell, nobody could tell me to go there.

Seeing that I ain't never died, I can't be afraid of something I never did.

I woke up about 4:30 in the morning. Something was happening. I was knocking on doors of the hotel, telling complete strangers I'd been born again. Some lady slammed the door in my face. I went to the next door and said, "I been born again!" They called security.

I think God chose to speak to me because I'm softhearted and he knew that I would be dumb enough to actually try.

Some people believe that fairness comes with obeying the rules. I'm one of those people.

I saw a tree standing that wouldn't sway with the wind. It stayed still. But one day a hurricane came and ripped it.

The woman had water or something in this pot. I said, "Mary, you gonna heat water or something?" She said, "I would never hurt you. I love you." I said, "Hurt me!?! I just wrote a song for you!" That's the furthest thing from my mind. I go back downstairs, I disrobe, I'm washing my face, and I feel this excruciating pain, and water or something flies all over the place. I get in the shower, cold water, and I'm screaming, and the next thing I hear is a shot fired and someone hit the floor. I loved her. I thought we could be together forever. She didn't mean it. I didn't know she had a problem.

Suicide is not an answer, it's destruction.

If I fast for forty days, I can go more places sitting right here on this couch than you could go in a jet plane.

The greatest thing that ever happened to me, to Al Green, the little boy from Arkansas, was that amidst all the doubts and speculation, I found peace.

INTERVIEWED BY LARRY GETLEN // **Photograph by Dana Lixenberg**

bio

BORN: Forrest City, Arkansas
April 13, 1946

> Green's first two albums, *Green Is Blues* (1970) and *Al Green Gets Next to You* (1971), firmly established his pop credentials.

> In 1974, Green's girlfriend poured boiling grits on his back while he was bathing, then shot herself. After undergoing a series of skin grafts, Green purchased a Memphis church and became an ordained minister.

> Another incident, a fall from a stage at a concert in Cincinnati in 1979, convinced him to abandon secular music. He turned exclusively to gospel music and religious pop and R & B.

> Green was inducted into the Rock and Roll Hall of Fame in 1995.

Willie Nelson

I am not a pig farmer. The pigs had a great time, but I didn't make any money.

I think I'm basically the same guy I always was. Maybe I've learned, through experience, to rein in some of the anger and temper they say redheads normally have. My grandmother used to tell me that a hard head makes a sore ass.

I believe that all roads lead to the same place—and that is wherever all roads lead to.

I like to play golf, but I don't play like Jack Nicklaus. I've been playing about twenty-five years. It's a difficult game to learn. You can't care too much. If you try too hard, you blow it. There's too much and too little. That's a good metaphor for a lot of things.

I don't think any person has any special knowledge about what God has planned for me and you any more than me and you do.

I started writing cheating songs when I was too young to have any idea what I was writing about—broken hearts and things like that. I just think it was something I already knew, something I had experienced in another lifetime.

We've already been reincarnated about a million times, maybe. It doesn't make sense any other way. How can we be created equal if there's a guy over here sitting on the corner, blind, with no feet, trying to make it, and there's another guy out there running around in a new Cadillac with two girls on either side of him and millions of dollars coming in?

A guy named Ben Dorsey used to work for Johnny Cash, and he had a bunch of suits that Johnny, had given him. He was walking down the street in Nashville in front of the Grand Ole Opry, and this guy came up with a guitar in his hand and thought Ben was one of the stars because he had on Cash's suit. He said, "How do you get started in this business?" And Ben said, "Ain't but one way, hoss. You start at the bottom, you go right to the top. Don't mess with that in-between shit."

Freedom is control in your own life. I have more control now than in the past, and I'm learning the value of saying no. That's very important.

Being open has helped me. With smoking pot or anything else. It's just a lot easier not to make excuses for who I am and what I do. It has to do with getting from point A to point B, retaining my sanity, and still progressing—taking some lemons and making some lemonade.

Contradiction exists in everyone. There's really nothing wrong with the fact that the same people who sing "Whiskey River" at the show tonight also sing "Amazing Grace." When I was back teaching Sunday school, I used to teach the same people on Sunday mornings that I sang to on Saturday nights. Nothing wrong with that, either.

If you start out looking at somebody, wondering whether he's good or bad, I think you're starting out in the wrong direction. 1 think we're all good and we're all bad.

Cruelty is all out of ignorance. If you knew what was in store for you, you wouldn't hurt anybody, because whatever you do comes back much more forceful than you send it out.

There is no such thing as an ex-wife. If you had a relationship, just because you don't live with them anymore doesn't mean that they're a non-human being, and if they want to say hello, then there should be a hello.

You could try to live monogamously. Good luck. There's people who say thinking about cheating is just as bad as doing it, so if you start looking at it from that angle, they got us all.

A wise man, Ray Price, told me recently that there's one thing he's learned in life. In fact, he called me on the phone to tell me this, and I said, "What is it?" He said, "Money makes women horny."

INTERVIEWED BY ROBERT HUBER // Photograph by Harry Benson

bio

BORN: Abbott, Texas
April 30, 1933

> Since releasing his first single in 1957, Nelson has created concept albums (his first, *Yesterday's Wine*, was recorded in 1971), gospel albums, jazz albums, movie soundtracks, myriad duet projects, Christmas albums, live albums, and an album of standards, *Stardust* (1978), which itself has become a standard.

> Nelson achieved superstar status in 1975 when he released *Red-Headed Stranger*. The record contained his first smash hit, a remake of Roy Acuff's "Blue Eyes Crying in the Rain."

> *Red-Headed Stranger* was so underproduced that the president of Columbia Records thought Nelson had presented him with a demo.

> Nelson has established himself as a champion for the family farmer with his annual Farm Aid concerts. Over the past decade, the charity has raised more than $12 million for a variety of rural American causes.

Elvis Presley

I wouldn't call girls a hobby. It's a pastime.

Any audience, as a rule, goes for a fast number.

I don't like to be called Elvis the Pelvis. It's one of the most childish expressions I've ever heard coming from an adult. But if they wanna call me that, there's nothin' I can do about it, so I just have to accept it. Just like you gotta accept the good with the bad, the bad with the good.

When I started singing, I weighed 153 pounds. I weigh 184 now. I haven't gotten any taller, but I'm putting on a little more weight.

I like pork chops and country ham, creamed potatoes, stuff like that. Redeye gravy. It comes from ham, bacon, stuff like that. It's the grease that you fry it in. I eat a lot of Jell-O. Fruit Jell-O.

I never have tasted alcohol.

In public, I like real conservative clothes, something that's not too flashy. But onstage, I like 'em as flashy as you can get 'em.

My mother goes to town now and she buys anything she wants, which makes me feel real good.

All my life, I've always had a nice time. We never had any money or nothin', but we never were hungry, you know. That's something to be thankful for.

The only exercise I get is on the stage. If I didn't get that, I'd get a little round around the tummy, as much as I eat.

The only kind of trouble I've ever been in is when I was stealing eggs when I was little. I think I know right from wrong.

I would like to learn how to act in the movies.

The thing I like about success is to know that you've got so many friends. A lot of real close friends that I've made since I've been in the business.

I don't think it's very good to work in your hometown.

I went into Sun Records and there was a guy in there took down my name, told me he might call me sometime. So he called me about a year and a half later, and I went in and made my first record, "That's All Right, Mama."

Some people tap their feet, some people snap their fingers, and some people just sway back and forth. I just started doin' my altogether, I guess.

bio

BORN: Tupelo, Mississippi, January 8, 1935
DIED: Graceland, Memphis, Tennessee
August 16, 1977

> Presley has sold over one billion records worldwide, more than any other artist. In the U.S., 148 of his albums and singles have gone gold, platinum or multi-platinum.
> He starred in 33 films and made history with his television appearances and specials.
> Among his many awards were 14 Grammy nominations (3 wins) and the Grammy Lifetime Achievement Award, which he received at age 36.
> Presley died in 1977 from an overdose of cocaine and barbituates.
> In 1982, his estate, Graceland, was opened to the public.
> The King lives on in the hearts of his fans, and in the form of postage stamps, velvet portraits, tabloid headlines, and professional imitators.

I watch my audience and listen to 'em, and I know that we're all getting somethin' out of our system. None of us knows what it is. The important thing is we're getting rid of it and nobody's getting hurt.

The first car I bought was the most beautiful car I've ever seen. It was secondhand, but I parked it outside of my hotel the day I got it. I sat up all night, just lookin' at it.

I haven't met *the* girl yet, but I will, and I hope I won't be too long, 'cause I get lonesome sometimes.

Critics have a job to do and they do it.

You have to put on a show for people in order to draw a crowd. If I just stood out there and sang and didn't move a muscle, then people would say, My goodness, I can stay home and listen to his records. You have to give them a show.

I hate to turn anybody down who wants an autograph.

The Colonel has a lot of friends in the entertainment business.

My mother never really wanted anything fancy. She just stayed the same all the way through the whole thing. I wish—there's a lot of things happened since she passed away that would've made her very happy and very proud. But that's life.

I'm not knocking people who like golf and tennis, but I like rugged sports—boxing, football, karate, things like that. I have a great ambition to play football. The thing I keep up with most is professional football. I know all the players, I know all their numbers.

I don't read any of the books that other people read. I read a lot of philosophy and some poetry. That type of stuff interests me.

I've had a pretty good lesson in human nature. It's more important to try to surround yourself with people who can give you a little happiness, because you only pass through this life once, Jack. You don't come back for an encore.

CULLED FROM PREVIOUSLY UNPUBLISHED INTERVIEWS, 1956 TO 1972, COURTESY RCA RECORDS
Photograph by Alfred Wertheimer

Lou Reed

You know the expression "God protects fools and drunks"? I qualify for both.

There are things I cannot even think of taking credit for. Pure luck. Dumb luck. Literally. I didn't get in the car. Or I moved two steps to the left. I could just as easily be in jail as be sitting here. I know that. A bad break—over and out. Luck.

Father of rap? No. Not for a second. If you do a monotone long enough, you suddenly have a name for it—it's suddenly "rap." I never thought of it that way myself.

I could be doing three or four albums a year. It's nothing to do one album; what do you do the rest of the time? I mean, it's not like it stops. It's always there, this racing around.

Everything's supposed to be grim, but there's another thing floating through a lot of [my work]. All the way back to the Velvets—some of that stuff's really funny, I think. It's not trendy, so I think it can withstand being heard years later. Many, many years. Which is part of the idea. I'm proud of it.

It's depressing when you're still around and your albums are out of print.

I can't do anything I want to. I mean, I can't have my own TV show. I can't have my own movie. But within my little world, nobody tells me what to put on the albums.

I always hear music in my head.

People say, "Do you keep these riffs and ideas and everything? Because then when you make a record, you could just go to the file cabinet." And I've always thought of doing something like that, but I don't. I just don't do it. I listen to these words flooding by, and once in a while, one just stays; it's very strange. I've learned not to even wonder about it anymore. Not that I give up; it's just, I don't understand it. I realize I don't understand it, and there you go.

You may be drawing a circle for the thousandth time, but maybe it's a slightly better circle.

It's appalling to me when there's a big miss, or the solution comes up two years after [an album] was out, and I say, "*Ohhh*, now you tell me." With any kind of luck, you get another crack at the ball.

There's a lot of songs people don't even notice that are my favorites, and they might come under the umbrella of "stupid." Like "Senselessly Cruel" and "Shooting Star"—I love that orchestral guitar at the beginning. It's one of the greatest things I ever did, and no one—zero—has ever noticed it.

That's the real secret of everything—rewriting. I always rewrite.

The fact that I haven't read every play by Shakespeare is depressing.

What I really want more than anything else is to quit smoking. That's what I want. I've quit a lot of things in my life, and this one's the worst. Maybe 'cause it's the last.

Have a good lawyer. Keep your hand on your wallet. The laws are unfair.

I've played basketball all my life. I love it. I don't play as much as I used to 'cause of my knees—they don't like jumping up and down—but I love basketball. The Knicks—I know certain people, and sometimes they let me have their tickets. And there I am: me, Spike, and Woody. But they don't put the camera on me.

Latrell Sprewell's had that burning thing. You have to think about choking the coach. Well, you know, you're a grown man, guy's standing there screaming at ya . . . Every guy makes mistakes. I'll speak for myself: I could be in that position. It would take me one second, where I could be in a situation like that.

You're a musician: You play. That's what you do.

INTERVIEWED BY SCOTT RAAB // Photograph by Len Irish

bio

BORN: Freeport, New York
March 2, 1942

> As a teenager, Reed learned guitar and recorded a doo-wop-inspired single with a band called The Shades. His parents were so worried that they forced him to undergo shock therapy.
> Reed began his career as lead guitarist of the influential art-rock quartet The Velvet Underground. Andy Warhol financed their first album, *Transformer* (1972), which was produced by David Bowie

and Mick Ronson. Reed wrote "Walk on the Wild Side," which became a radio classic in the U.S. and made Reed a bona fide star in the U.K.
> Soon after he went solo and recorded the extremely dark album *Berlin* (1973), which was about a love affair between two junkies. It reached the Top 10 in Britain, but did not chart in the U.S. In 1974, he released *Sally Can't Dance*, a pop metal album, and finally won over a large U.S. following.
> While many of Reed's songs deal with his depression and heroin addiction, he gave up drugs in the early '80s and staged a comeback with the acclaimed *Blue Mask* (1982).

Lucinda Williams

There's this whole myth that surrounds the idea of songwriting—you know, you're sitting on the edge of your bed, drinking Jack Daniel's, depressed as shit, and you're writing. That's never worked for me.

Some of my best friends are music critics.

The perfect man? A poet on a motorcycle. You know, the kind who lives on the edge, the free spirit. But he's also gotta have the soul of a poet and a brilliant mind. So, you know, good luck.

I don't endorse organized religion by any means.

I love that Bob Dylan song "Ramona." I *love* that song. "Ramona, come closer, shut softly your watery eyes." *Watery eyes.* That's writing. And that's what's missing in a lot of writing today. People would just say "eyes" instead of "watery eyes."

In a perfect world, I'd just run up onto the stage with no makeup on.

There are good people everywhere. Even in the music industry.

It's easier to write songs when you're single.

I don't have the vocal range that I'd like to have. That's one of the reasons that I started writing songs. I didn't want to be seen as a singer. I figured if I wrote my own songs, my voice wouldn't be the main focal point.

I'm not used to getting asked these kinds of questions.

If you're a dreamer and a romantic, you're going to have a hard time in the world. That's all there is to it. Because it's just a rough, hard world. I try to find bits of joy where I can. I'm trying to find a way to find some peace. I'm almost desperate. I don't want to be miserable the rest of my life, you know.

I haven't decided yet how I feel about reincarnation. But as my dad always used to remind me, I was born the same month and year Hank Williams died. January '53.

The Pentagon basically controls everything.

Why should I listen to … *whatever* when I can listen to John Coltrane?

My father didn't raise his voice. I didn't get disciplined in the traditional sense, and a lot of times I wish I had. I wished he'd just yell and get it over with, like the other kids' parents. But it was this kind of stern, serious look into your eyes, and this *Do you realize what you've done?* With me, it had to do with not wanting to disappoint. And there's a lot more power to that than, you know, the Archie Bunker way of discipline.

bio

BORN: Lake Charles, Louisiana
January 26, 1953

> Williams's 1988 self-titled album blended country, blues, and folk; tracks from this record would eventually be covered by Tom Petty, Mary-Chapin Carpenter, and Patty Loveless.
> Though signed by RCA, she left the label without releasing a record, preferring the creative control offered by the indie label Chameleon, which issued the album *Sweet Old World* in 1992.
> She won a Grammy in 1998 for *Car Wheels on a Gravel Road,* which was both a commercial and critical success.

The natural state of humans is the way we are when we're children. Before we get infiltrated with all this junk.

You can be in hell and create your own heaven. But it takes an immense amount of discipline.

The night after September 11, my tour manager went out and bought an American flag and put it up onstage. I didn't want it to be on the stage, though, when I was playing. I'd have felt more comfortable with a peace symbol up there, or maybe a big peace symbol over the flag. I let him keep it there, but I felt uncomfortable about it, and it made some of the other guys in the band uncomfortable, too. Everybody's got their own private feelings about these things.

Apathy and complacency are the kiss of death. There's just no excuse for that.

Children? Either I wasn't with the right person, or the timing wasn't right: It just wasn't all there together for me for it to happen. I've never been pregnant, so I don't even know. Maybe I can't even get pregnant. How do I know? I don't even know!

I'm drawn to bass players, and I haven't really figured out why. They tend to be more in the background and kind of holding the beat. Sometimes lead-guitar players can be frustrated singer-songwriters. They really want to be in the spotlight. But bass players, they've got that rhythmic thing. That beat, you know? There's something about that rhythm section.

The things that are perfect are the things we don't have any control over.

I remember feeling different from the other kids.

INTERVIEWED BY BRENDAN VAUGHAN // **Photograph by Michael Halisbrand**

The Loudmouths

Muhammad Ali

F. Lee Bailey

Mario Batali

Robert Evans

Larry King

Bill O'Reilly

Don Rickles

Roseanne

George Steinbrenner

Muhammad Ali

Heavyweight
Berrien Springs, Michigan

God will not place a burden on a man's shoulders knowing that he cannot carry it.

Parkinson's is my toughest fight. No, it doesn't hurt. It's hard to explain. I'm being tested to see if I'll keep praying, to see if I'll keep my faith. All great people are tested by God.

The sun is always shining someplace.

I came back to Louisville after the Olympics with my shiny gold medal. Went into a luncheonette where black folks couldn't eat. Thought I'd put them on the spot. I sat down and asked for a meal. The Olympic champion wearing his gold medal. They said, "We don't serve niggers here." I said, "That's okay, I don't eat 'em." But they put me out in the street. So I went down to the river, the Ohio River, and threw my gold medal in it.

Since that day, things in America have changed 100 percent.

When you're right, nobody remembers. When you're wrong, nobody forgets.

Silence is golden when you can't think of a good answer.

We have one life / It soon will be past / What we do for God / Is all that will last.

Goodness? My mother.

When your mother dies, it really hurts. But with time, you get used to it. That's nature's way.

My definition of evil is unfriendliness.

The best way to make your dreams come true is to wake up.

Comedy is a funny way of being serious. My way of joking is to tell the truth. That's the funniest joke in the world.

It's possible for the heavyweight champion of the world to be with one woman.

Love is a net that catches hearts like fish.

Rubble is trouble.

The more we help others, the more we help ourselves.

I like Joe.

Watching George come back to win the title got me all excited. Made me want to come back. But then the next morning came, and it was time to start running. I lay back in bed and said, "That's okay, I'm still the Greatest."

If I could meet anybody? The prophet Muhammad.

I'm most proud of my family.

Enjoy your children, even when they don't act the way you want them to.

Lighting that torch in Atlanta didn't make me nervous. Standing up to the government—*that* made me nervous.

Wisdom is knowing when you can't be wise.

The one thing I don't understand is war.

Brooding over blunders is the biggest blunder.

I'd like to live to a hundred.

I just wish people would love everybody else the way that they love me. It would be a better world.

INTERVIEWED BY CAL FUSSMAN // **Photograph by Neil Leifer**

BORN: Louisville, Kentucky
January 17, 1942

> Birth name: Cassius Marcellus Clay, Jr.
> Heavyweight prizefighter, antiwar protester, and international ambassador of goodwill. Ali's extroverted, colorful style, both in and out of the ring, heralded a new type of media-conscious celebrity athlete.

> As the dominant heavyweight boxer of the '60s and '70s, he won an Olympic gold medal, captured the professional world heavyweight championship on three separate occasions, and successfully defended his title 19 times.
> Through his bold assertions of black pride, his conversion to the Muslim faith, and his outspoken opposition to the Vietnam War, Ali became a highly controversial figure during the '60s. At the height of his fame, he was described as "the most recognizable human being on earth."

F. Lee Bailey

Attorney
West Palm Beach, Florida

I've never regretted getting anyone out of jail.

I'm slow to accept assertions simply because somebody made them. On the other hand, I'm inclined to trust people until they give me a reason not to.

I've had three divorces. All were accomplished without the need of a lawyer.

Sex has caused at least half the problems my clients have suffered over the years.

There are always too many lawyers; there are never enough good ones.

I'd have to go down as an agnostic. If you had to prove the existence of a supreme being in a court of law, the question would be, could you enter the Bible as evidence? Then, could you *prove* it?

I never take a note during a trial. I like to throw direct quotes at a witness: "Did you say this? And I quote . . . " If he says no, I'll say, "Do you realize that you said just that on page so-and-so?" He realizes that I've just quoted him directly without having a piece of paper in front of me. After a while, the witness gets frightened. He says, "I'm not sure." So I pull out the paper. At the end of the day, if he's a sneaky witness, I might give him a quote he *didn't* say, and he'll adopt it: "Yeah, I think I said that." I did that once with the chairman of the board for a big bank. He adopted a quote he never said and admitted liability. The case settled the next day.

BORN: Waltham, Massachusetts
June 10, 1933

> As a young man, Bailey joined the U.S. Marine Corps, where he served as a jet fighter pilot and legal officer. He logged more than 15,000 flying hours as an officer and civilian pilot while attending Harvard University.
> He was valedictorian of his class at Boston University Law School.
> Bailey has defended numerous high-profile clients including Samuel Sheppard, the doctor accused of murdering his wife and the inspiration for the television series and movie *The Fugitive*. He also assisted Robert Shapiro in the defense of O. J. Simpson.
> Bailey's three nonfiction books, *The Defense Never Rests*, *For the Defense*, and *Cleared for the Approach*, are all best-sellers.

Not only does the Atkins diet work, but you can eat all the butter you like.

Fear is something you have to throw into a corner. Constantly. Because it never goes away.

Nobody is born with an expertise in sex any more than they're born to be a good witness. They have to be taught.

Truth makes me think of a parachute rigger. The rigger is the guy who stuffs the parachutes. In my day, a pilot always wore a parachute, and the rigger's name was always on it. That way, the pilot could hand it to the rigger at any time and make him jump.

I'm satisfied that O. J. didn't do it.

People ask how I do all the things I do. They say, "How do you find the time?" Time is an elusive concept. There is no time to find. People who are busy *make* time, they don't find it.

My parents divorced when I was eight years old. At the time, I thought that they had done us a disservice. But as you grow up, you realize that you're not the only consideration.

Five hours a night has always been adequate.

Every son has a busy father and doesn't get the attention he deserves.

Because of my military training, I had no difficulty disciplining myself to live within the parameters imposed upon me when I was recently in jail.

When I was three years old, I was crying about not being able to get a tricycle—this was during the Depression—and my mother said, "You'll get anything you want in this world if you work hard enough for it. And if you don't get it, stand in front of the mirror and ask yourself why. The answer will be looking right at you."

There are two lawyers in a case. One of them thinks he's got a bad case. That lawyer wants no one on the jury with an IQ in three figures.

You can whack me once in the back, and I can take it. But that's the last time it'll ever happen.

Laughing juries don't convict.

INTERVIEWED BY CAL FUSSMAN // Photograph by Max Aguilera-Hellweg

Mario Batali

Chef
New York City

God is fat. God's also skinny. God's also Linda Evangelista. God's a lot of things.

Who ordered all this stuff? Oh, yeah. Me.

Food is much better off the hand than the fork.

My first memory? I can't remember. But I can remember being almost five, sitting on a swing, and wondering how many times I was going to sit on a swing in my life. Of course I didn't realize it at that moment, but what I was really wondering was, How long can I stay young?

I can tell in two minutes if I should hire someone in the kitchen. *Two* minutes. It's his desire. It's that open-eyed, attentive expression. If he doesn't have it . . . I mean, I can teach a chimp how to cook dinner. But I cannot teach a chimp how to love it.

I come from an Italian family. One of the greatest and most profound expressions we would ever use in conversations or arguments was a slamming door. The slamming door was our punctuation mark.

If you want your kids to listen to you, don't yell at them. Whisper. Make them lean in. My kids taught me that. And I do it with adults now.

What do I love about New York? Eight million people can hate my restaurant, and there's still eight million left! Not that I want to piss anyone off. But it gives you a lot of chances to work on your game.

I don't know about those personal trainers. They seem to be for people who don't have enough domination in their lives.

A little piece of watermelon on top of a magnificent piece of raw tuna in the middle of summer makes a lot of sense—as long as you put some salt on it.

Have I ever seen it on somebody's face? Oh, yeah. The worst case was Gael Greene, *New York* magazine food critic. I'm working at a place called Rocco's in the Village. We were kind of warned that she was coming in, and we were ready. I'm cooking with one other guy. Six people order appetizers. *Boom. Boom. Boom.* Steamed mussels. I'm putting them all on the plate, and as they're going out, I get a whiff. Something's wrong. These mussels smell like shit. It wasn't that they were spoiled; they were in their mating season. They give off this weird smell. I go running out after them just as they're placed in front of her. She smells them and just waves them away. God, I'll never forget it.

Holding back is the hardest thing for a cook to do, especially in a multicourse meal. Because the cook is battling what makes him a great cook. The cook wants to *give*. Here it is! And that's a hard thing to control. You don't realize that by seven courses, the diner's ready to vomit.

You sit down at Katz's and you eat the big bowl of pickles and you're eating the pastrami sandwich, and halfway through you say to yourself, I should really wrap this up and save it for tomorrow. But the sandwich is calling you: *Remember the taste you just had. So fatty. It's what you want. It's what you are!* I've never gotten home from Katz's with a doggie bag in my hand. A pastrami sandwich at Katz's is what's bad and good about food. It's the sacred and the profane.

Escarole in December is not escarole in January.

Flexibility, tolerance, thoughtfulness, love—that's what makes a marriage work. But love goes away quickly when kids are around for a while. There are going to be days when the love in your relationship becomes a secondary factor. It'll come back. So you hold on. What choice do you have?

It's not like I'm megalomaniacally opening up restaurants. The truth is, I can't stop. Because ever since I've been in New York City, which is twelve years, every time I've run into a good person, I've said, "Stick with me and one day you'll get a slice of the pie." At this point, the slices are starting to be handed out. I'm like an Italian grandmother who's been watching her grandchildren learn to ride on the old family bicycle. When they can ride it with no hands, they're ready for a new bike.

If you're smart, then your dreams evolve, too.

My last meal? The food would be much less significant than the company.

You want a little more wine?

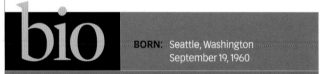

bio

BORN: Seattle, Washington
September 19, 1960

> Mario's celebrated restaurant, Babbo Ristorante e Enoteca, was the first in an ever-expanding list of New York City hotspots specializing in innovative Italian fare. Most recent additions are the Barcelona-inspired eateries Casa Mono and Bar Jamon.

> A mainstay of the television Food Network, Mario is host of *Molto Mario, Mario Eats Italy, Ciao America* and, most recently, *Mediterranean Mario*.

> His books include *Simple Italian Food* (1998), *Mario Batali Holiday Food* (2000), and *The Babbo Cookbook* (2002). In 2002, he was named Best Chef in New York City by the James Beard Foundation.

INTERVIEWED BY CAL FUSSMAN // Photograph by Michael Lewis

Robert Evans

Cojones! Either you're born with 'em or without 'em. Mine have done me as much harm as good. They've given me an interesting life. But it's much easier to read about it than to live it.

Someone once told me that the three most dangerous things in life are your own mouth, someone else's mouth, and a car. Adding a cell phone to the mix can only lead to disaster.

If you're a good-looking guy who likes dames and lives a cavalier life, your peers will not wish you success.

Fuck 'em. Fuck 'em all.

Background makes foreground. This goes for movies, it goes for dressing, it goes for living. Here's an example: If I go to a party and eight different people come over to me and say, "Gee, that's a great-looking tie," as soon as I get home, I take the tie off and put it in the shredder. Screw the tie! I'm not there to make the *tie* look good. The tie is there to make *me* look good. That's what I mean by background makes foreground.

The only way you can make a deal is if you're ready to blow it.

Rejection breeds obsession.

I guess I'm an old-fashioned guy, but I like to look into somebody's eyes.

I was forced to use the name Evans. My father had a great disdain for his father. His father was a degenerate gambler. Used to go out for lunch and come back a month and a half later with no money. My father had to quit school and work to support his family. My father said to my brother and I, "Both you boys are going to be very successful. I don't want you to carry on my father's name. If you have success, I want my mother to get the credit." Her name was Evan.

Instant gratification takes too long.

The only time I sensed peace of mind was when I had a stroke five years ago. Honest to God. I was here at home with Wes Craven. I'd never met him before, and I wanted to buy his new novel. I was making a toast, and the champagne flute dropped out of my hand and I fell to the floor. It was like I was dead. I scared the *shit* out of the King of Scream. I'm lying there, and the paramedic comes to see if I'm dead, and I look up and manage to say the only thing that could be said at that moment. I said to Wes: "I told you it's never dull around here." I was in total peace. Not in pain. I was dying, and I saw the flash of the ambulance, and I knew I was taking a trip. I woke up fifteen hours later, looking at the white ceiling, and I thought I'd made heaven. But I wasn't dead. And I wasn't Robert Evans, either. I was Quasimodo. I was totally paralyzed.

Royalty fades but infamy stays.

I've been shot down, bloodied, trampled, accused, disgraced, threatened, betrayed, scandalized, maligned. . . . Not that I'm complaining.

If you go by the rules, you end up being an accountant.

I don't kiss and tell. I learned early in life that continued silence is the greatest insurance policy to continued breathing.

The Cotton Club? I'll say this: It was the single biggest mistake of my entire life. I spent six years on it, and I never even went to the opening. It was looked upon as a bomb. And to me it *was* a bomb. It destroyed my life. Not long after, my accountant got on the phone and said, "You've got to do something because the IRS is going to take the house." He said, "You got thirty-seven dollars to your name." I couldn't even meet Friday's payroll, and the terrible thing about it is that I wasn't even worried. I knew I'd make something happen. And I did. That comes from cojones. That comes from being in a bullring and seeing the horns come at you. I shit in my pants, but I stayed there.

I should, by all reason, be dead. But I'm not dead. I'm five years old. Hey, I can either be five or seventy-two. Being five is the better choice.

INTERVIEWED BY CAL FUSSMAN // Photograph by Gregg Segal

bio

BORN: New York, New York
June 29, 1930

> Birth name: Robert J. Shapera
> Evans was appointed head of production at the floundering Paramount Pictures in 1966. Under his watch, the rejuvenated studio turned out major hits including *Rosemary's Baby* (1968) and *The Godfather* (1972).
> Evans's first film as executive producer was Roman Polanski's *Chinatown* (1974). He also helped resurrect John Travolta's career with the trend-setting production *Urban Cowboy* (1980).
> *The Kid Stays in the Picture,* a documentary about Evans's life in movies, opened to rave reviews in 2002 and became an art house success. Most recently, Evans created and produced the animated series *Kid Notorious* for Comedy Central.

Larry King

I gambled only on horses. I liked the thrill of them turning into the stretch. I still like it. Except it's not as much fun when you don't need the money. It's much more fun when you're riding on the rent.

The best day I ever had at the track—it could never fit the way you do this story, because it's a whole magazine piece. I'm dead broke. Station I was working at had just switched to ethnic. Hired all black—and we were all let go at once. So I'm out of work. I have forty-eight dollars to my name. It's late May, and I'm paid through the end of May rent. I got a daughter I'm trying to support. I'm divorced. It's 1972. I drive to Calder racetrack. I'm sitting there and it's the third race and I look up at the horses. I see a horse called Lady Forli. It's a filly running against males. Normally, fillies don't beat males. We're talking cheap horses. I look up at the board and she's 70 to 1. I look at the guy next to me and say, "You know, this horse, three races back, won in more or less the same company. Why is she 70 to 1?" Guy says, "Well, there's a couple of new horses here." I said, "Yeah, but she should be, like, 20 to 1, not 70 to 1." Screw it. I bet ten dollars on the horse to win. I keep looking at the horse. The more I'm looking at this horse, the more I like it. So I now bet exactas. I bet it on top of every other horse and below every other horse— 11 over everybody and 11 under everybody. Now I've got a wheel. It's called a wheel. Oh—I'm wearing a Pierre Cardin jean outfit that has no pockets. The keys are in the car where the valet parked it. So I said, "Wait a minute. I got four dollars left. I gotta give the valet two bucks. I've got my cigarettes—don't need money for that. You could also bet a trifecta." So my birthday is November 19. The horse is number 11. So I'll bet 11-1-9. Now I've got 11 on top, I've got 11 on bottom, I've got 11 to win, and I've got a trifecta 11-1-9. I've got two dollars left to my name. Now the race begins. They break out of the gate, the 1 breaks on top, the 9 is second, and the 11 is third. The 11 passes the 9, the 11 passes the 1, and they run in a straight line all around the track. No question. The 11 wins by five lengths. The 1 is three lengths ahead of the 9. So I've got every winning ticket. I got it to win. I got the exacta. I got the trifecta. I collect $11,000—*eleven thousand dollars*! But I got no pockets. So I stuff all the money in my jacket. I don't know what to do with it. I run outta the track. The valet guy comes out and brings me the car. He says, "You leaving so early?" I said, "Yeah." He says, "Bad day, Mr. King?" I tip him fifty dollars. Guy nearly faints. I gotta go somewhere. I drove into a vacant lot which is now Joe Robbie Stadium. I parked among the weeds. And I opened up my jacket and all the money spilled out. I counted out $11,000. You know what I did? My child support was $100 a month. I sent $1,200. My rent was $360 a month. I paid my rent for a year. I bought twenty cartons of cigarettes, stacked 'em up in my apartment. And that may have been the happiest moment of my life. Now, today, if I go to the track and win $11,000, it's very nice, but it won't affect my life one iota. It's nice to win. But when you *really* need it . . .

The truth about foxhole humor is it's never funny when it's happening.

I have more faith in myself on the air than off.

I love bums. Bums in New York are literate bums. Bums in New York could run a grocery chain in Des Moines.

There's no trick to being yourself.

A sense of humor is a major aphrodisiac. I'm certainly an average-looking guy, but I've had some *very* nice women in my life. I always could make 'em laugh.

A good ensemble—tie and suspenders—should be about $200.

Once the mind gets curious, no law can stop it.

"Why?" is a great question for a talk-show host because it can't be answered in one word.

You always remember the date of your heart attack.

I'm not an atheist because that's a religion.

Retire? To what?

INTERVIEWED BY CAL FUSSMAN // Photograph by Michael Lavine

Bill O'Reilly

There's no excuse for eating rice cakes at any time. It's like eating dust. What are they doing here?

Never been with a hooker, never been on a blind date. My ego's too big.

Yes, I get angry when the federal government spends $100,000 on a study to find out why people don't like beets. I wouldn't mind paying 60 percent of every dollar I make in taxes if I was helping somebody in the street who wants to clean up his life, or giving some kid a school lunch and an after-school program. I'm more than happy to do that. It's a philosophical thing. If I work hard for my money, I don't want to see it wasted.

Dr. Spock was lucky he never met William O'Reilly Sr. There would have been violence.

I was never aimless. I always had a very centered existence. That's what Catholic school gave me.

My father didn't take any risks. And he paid a big, big price for it. I used to see him come home every day. I don't know how he did it. Left every morning at 6:30, and he was home every evening at 6:30. He was bean counting. He was unhappy, and it ruined him. I learned a lot from watching him. He got beaten down by the system, and I said, I'm never going to let that system beat me. If I think I can do something, I'm going to do it.

If you're gonna swagger, it's better to be big.

On television, people respond to my definite view of the world.

There are some issues that have gray areas—abortion is one of them. But I do believe that 90 percent of the world's problems are black-and-white.

I'm not right-wing, I'm not left-wing. I want to get the best solution to the problem and use the solution that works. That drives people crazy because they try to pin an ideology on you.

Bobby Kennedy was the most effective politician I've ever seen. I mean, he wiped out the Mafia. Nobody wanted him to do it. But those guys just pissed him off and he said, I want these guys *out*. And he did it. Single-handedly. Now, why did he do it? He's a rich guy. They don't have any impact on his life—Hoffa and those guys had no impact at all. They were actually helping his brother. What was it inside him that made him do it? I'd like to talk to him about that.

You can't ever wipe out evil. But it's like this: If someone comes to your house bent on killing you or your family, what do you do? You don't negotiate with them. You don't try to understand why they're coming to kill you and your family. You *kill* them. That's what you do.

I had rules. I would never sleep with any girl who was drunk or high. And believe me, in the sixties and the seventies, I lost a lot of opportunities. But again, the ego. I wanted them to say, "Hey, O'Reilly, c'mon in here." I didn't want them staggering in, saying, "What's your name?" That wasn't going to do it for me.

The best partners are the ones who can live life on their own.

You will never teach your kid anything more important than discipline.

Disco? I didn't have a white suit or anything like that. And I wasn't running around with Bianca Jagger. I'd just show up, get out on the dance floor, and fake it. The soundtrack to *Saturday Night Fever* was pretty good. I like Evelyn "Champagne" King. My wife gives me such a hard time when she sees me teach my little daughter all the disco songs. She knows the booty song. KC and the Sunshine Band. You know, *Shake shake shake . . . shake shake shake . . . shake your boooooooty.*

If you don't care what other people think of you, you can feel comfortable anywhere.

Americans never want to die. They're afraid to die. Everybody thinks that if they eat sandwiches with sprouts in them, they're going to squeeze out another three or four years. You know what? I'd rather die three or four years earlier than eat the sprouts. I don't go for that California stuff. I get the Boar's Head. Have them slap that ham on there. I'll go for lettuce and tomato once in a while, but you gotta get my permission to put that stuff on first.

INTERVIEWED BY CAL FUSSMAN // Photograph by Nigel Parry

bio

BORN: Levittown, New York
September 10, 1949

> Just three weeks after joining *Inside Edition* as a correspondent in 1989, O'Reilly became the anchor.

> In 1996, he joined the Fox News Channel as the anchor-host of *The O'Reilly Factor*, now the most-watched program on cable news.
> O'Reilly has written two books, *The O'Reilly Factor* and *The No Spin Zone*, both of which reached number one on the *New York Times* best-seller list.
> He has estimated that he receives around 30,000 e-mails a day.

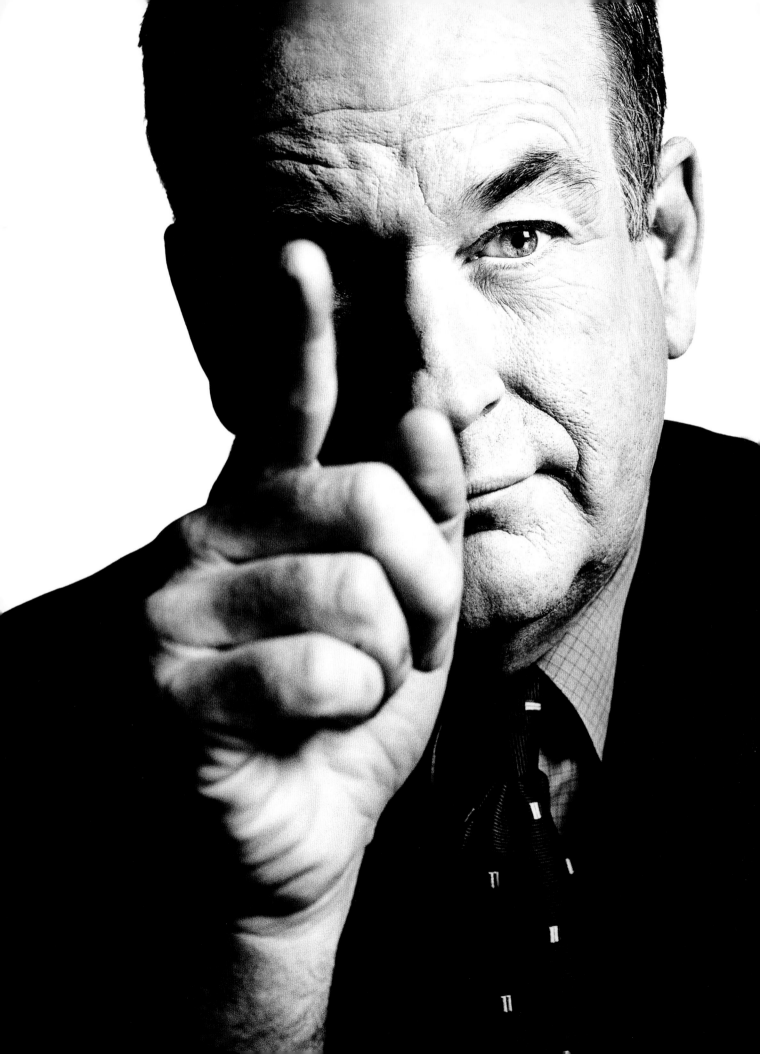

Don Rickles

No matter where you go in this world, you will always find a Jew sitting in the beach chair next to you.

When you stand alone and sell yourself, you can't please everyone. But when you're different, you can last.

Famous people are deceptive. Deep down, they're just regular people. Like Larry King. We've been friends for forty years. He's one of the few guys I know who's *really* famous. One minute he's talking to the president on his cell phone, and then the next minute he's saying to me, Do you think we ought to give the waiter another dollar?

Sex is great, but when you get to be my age, you've got to pace it a little bit. Otherwise you get tired.

I don't have regrets. I've never sat here and thought, Gee, if only I'd done *The Man Who Came to Dinner* on Broadway, I would have been happier.

You can't study comedy; it's within you. It's a personality. My humor is an attitude.

The thing I love about Vegas is that it's a melting pot. It's like working Ellis Island.

Once in a while, when I'm alone, I think about my age. I think, How many more years do I have on this earth? But I can't really conceive of dying. Somehow, in my head, I don't think I'll die. I know that everybody dies, of course. I just think that it'll never come to me. It's crazy, but there it is.

People think being in your seventies means sitting around in a chair with a blanket over your legs, drooling.

I can sit all day in a comfortable chair and watch ball games, but I don't need a blanket.

I've got an accountant who's been with me forty years. If he makes a mistake, he dies.

BORN: New York, New York
May 8, 1926

> An ad-libber, Rickles was considered "too hot to handle" until his freewheeling appearance on Johnny Carson's *Tonight Show* in 1965 brought him industry acclaim and national attention.
> His voice has been featured in the animated hits *Toy Story* (1996) and *Toy Story 2* (1999). He has also played dramatic roles, notably in Martin Scorsese's film *Casino* (1995).
> Rickles has been voted among the nation's best-dressed men by the Custom Tailors Guild of America and the Tailors Council of America.

Showbiz is great if you're successful.

Struggling is hard because you never know what's at the end of the tunnel.

I don't feel an obligation to give everyone a hard time, but when they're important people, it's fun. I've met every president since Gerald Ford. When you go in the reception line and they announce your name, they all look at me the same way. They all go, Oh, *nooooooo*! You can see it in their eyes. They're like, Oh, Jesus, he's gonna say something! Here I am, this little Jew from the neighborhood, and the president of the United States is cowering. Now *that's* entertainment!

Asians are nice people, but they burn a lot of shirts.

Political correctness? In my humor, I never talk about politics. I was never much into all that.

I don't care if the average guy on the street really knows what I'm like, as long as he knows I'm not really a mean, vicious guy. My friends and family know what I'm really like. That's what's important.

Hollywood has changed. It's not glamorous like the old days. Last time my wife and I went down there to go to the movies, we got car-jacked by a guy with a .357 Magnum.

I've never walked offstage and said, "I shouldn't have done that." Because when you do what I do, you're like a fighter. You throw the right hand and say, "That's what got me to this dance." You can't have doubt. If you have doubt, there's no show.

It's tough having the last name Rickles. Luckily, my kids handled it great.

I used to play golf. I wanted to be a better player, but after a while I realized I'd always stink. And that's when I really started to enjoy the game.

Room service is great if you want to pay $500 for a club sandwich.

One time I did Carson and I made a joke about a black guy in the audience, and Carson stopped me and said, "Show me a black guy." The camera panned the audience, and there was no black guy. And I said to Johnny, "Did they laugh?" The answer was yes. And that's all that matters.

I always rib people, but nobody ever gives me a hard time. I don't know why. Maybe they're afraid of what I might say. There's probably a lesson in that somewhere, but I don't know what it is.

The old days were the old days. And they were great days. But now is now.

INTERVIEWED BY MIKE SAGER //Photograph by Peggy Sirota

Roseanne

Entertainer
Lake Arrowhead, California

Men are very fragile.

Everything is a government conspiracy.

If you think you're getting bad love, that means you're giving it, too.

Self-esteem is the goddamn root of all evil.

Those who can't do, teach. And, as Woody Allen says, those who can't teach, teach gym. And, as I say, those who can't teach gym become experts. That's who we look to for answers these days—the biggest friggin' idiots in the world. People who have never had kids telling you how to raise yours. Gay people telling you how to make your marriage work. Men telling women how to raise their self-esteem. The only thing that cures everything is talking to people who have the same problem you do. The rest is just a moneymaking bullshit scheme that some asshole is getting rich on.

One of my missions on earth is to tell people how full of shit they are.

I'm from the streets, but I'm also very gracious. They always leave that part out.

I used to think that people liked you if you told the truth.

Women love to lose themselves in effect. Men love to lose themselves in cause.

When you grow up Jewish, your parents are always telling you, Nobody's better than you. Then, usually when you're about sixteen, they start telling you that you're no better than anybody else. That's the whole thing about being Jewish: It's too hot, but it's too cold. You don't want your kids to be certain of anything. If you're certain of anything, that's when you get into trouble. That's the lesson of the Jews.

You have to participate in a marriage. That was news to me.

The hardest thing I ever learned about being a wife was that I'm not the husband.

The wife is the one who serves. But she is also the one who rules. It's weird, because you have to stay humble and be strong all at the same time. The husband? He serves, too, only in a different way. And he protects. Just like the LAPD.

The object of business is to keep your buddies working, even if they're fuckin' idiots.

I realized very early in my life that the rest of the world marched to the beat of a different drummer than I did. But I felt sorry for them. I thought I was the only one who was right. And I think that's what probably saved my life—being that deluded.

Fame makes you a target, but it also allows you to put your ethics into play.

I'm way funnier in the morning.

Our world today is all about things rather than ideas. It's vanquishment by enticement.

Nobody repays any debts in Hollywood. Until you're dead. Then they give you the Thalberg Award.

You're as sick as your secrets.

Del Taco has the best fast food. Wendy's has the best fries. I don't like McDonald's anymore; it's just cardboard. Burger King at least has mayonnaise. Taco Bell is great, 'cause you can't eat Del Taco every time.

Diets are the root of all evil. They are the reason everyone is fat.

I hate sex. I'm done with it. I tell my husband he should go have sex with other people, but he never does. I don't know why. Probably because I told him to. Whatever you tell men, they always do the opposite. The trick is to tell them they should cheat on you, and then don't have sex with them, either. Then you have a happy marriage. You stop having sex and just hang out and eat and watch TV.

Women's problem with sex is simple: We don't like having sex with someone we know too well.

Inner peace means inner silence.

I'm tired of asking anymore. I'm just doing.

INTERVIEWED BY MIKE SAGER // Photograph by Peggy Sirota

bio

BORN: Salt Lake City, Utah
November 3, 1952

> Roseanne established her distinctive comic persona as the star, writer, and producer of her hit TV show, *Roseanne*. The series enjoyed a nine-year run on ABC and redefined the way middle-class American families could be portrayed on television.

> Her autobiographies, *Roseanne: My Life as a Woman* (1992) and *My Lives* (1994), were both best-sellers.

> She recently set up the Roseanne Foundation, a nonprofit organization that raises funds to develop and support programs for dealing with the effects of child abuse.

George Steinbrenner

If you haven't got a hernia yet, you ain't pulling your share.

I defy anyone to eat a powdered jelly doughnut without getting some of it on them. Not that it stops me from trying.

Before every home World Series game, I walk the restrooms of Yankee Stadium to make sure they're clean.

It thrills me to sing the national anthem.

There are few people who can say they're the only one. My dad was one of those people. He was six feet four. German. Very strong willed. He went to MIT. Not only was he at the top of his naval-architecture class, but he was the only national collegiate champion MIT ever had—an outstanding hurdler. He pushed me to strive for excellence. If I competed in five races and won four, we talked about the one I lost.

My mother was Irish. She couldn't do enough good for others. If I have any strain in me that drives me to try to help others, she's where it comes from.

What do I love about my wife? Well, she's put up with me all these years. And I'm not an easy person to live with.

Don't just drink from the gymnasium fountain. Drink from every fountain on campus.

When you're entrusted with a tradition, you've got to protect it.

My dad never let me have an allowance. He gave me chickens. I had to feed them, gather the eggs, and sell them. I kept ledgers. I had to run it like a business. When I went off to military school, I sold the business to my sisters for too much, and they haven't liked me since.

It's not right to say, "Send Darryl Strawberry to prison." What did he do? Did he hold up a gas station? Did he shoot anybody? He has a sickness. A disease. You can't tell it to stop. If you want to go after people, go after the goddamn people who're selling the stuff.

Robert Merrill will sing the national anthem at Yankee Stadium as long as he can move.

What happened in Cleveland will eventually happen to Yankee Stadium. We grow. We can hold on to traditions in certain ways, but we can't hold on to all of it forever. Look at the restrooms at Yankee Stadium: They're not good enough anymore. I go to the World Series at Yankee Stadium and see a long line of guys waiting to get into the men's room. Waiting! All I can do is say, "Hey, guys, hang tough!"

I don't want to see Yankees with long hair. I don't go for that crap.

Having people scream nasty things at you is part of sports. I've had my share of it. They pay their money, they can say what they want.

When it comes to hiring, number one for me is loyalty. I want a person who's devoted to the task.

Why should there be any such thing as a kid "at risk" in this country? If they're at risk, then we're not doing our job.

The rate of the pack is determined by the speed of the leader.

bio

BORN: Rocky River, Ohio
July 4, 1930

> Steinbrenner earned his fortune as owner and chief operating officer of the American Shipbuilding Company in Cleveland.
> In 1973, he became the principal owner of the New York Yankees. At the time, he knew nothing about baseball.
> He has fired at least 17 managers.
> Under his reign, the Yankees have won six World Series.

New Yorkers are strong people. They've got to fight in the morning to get a cab. They go to a lunch place at noon, they gotta fight to get a table or a stool off the counter. You have to give the city a team that's filled with battlers.

Joe Torre is special to me. He was fired in three places before we hired him. The Mets had fired him. People said he didn't know what he was doing. There was a headline in the *Daily News:* CLUELESS JOE. I never let him forget that.

Patton had his shortcomings: He couldn't get along with the others. But every time they got in trouble, who'd they turn to?

Second place is really the first loser.

I never ask a man to work harder than I work.

My grandchildren can get away with anything around me.

There are people who probably call me Boss as a joke. But most of the people who call me that, it's *respect.*

Lead, follow, or get the hell out of the way.

INTERVIEWED BY CAL FUSSMAN // Photograph by Harry Benson

The Mavericks

Chuck Barris

Richard Branson

Conrad Dobler

Larry Flynt

Lauren Hutton

Evel Knievel

Suge Knight

Gene Simmons

Ike Turner

Ted Williams

Chuck Barris

I had a pillow in my bedroom that said NO REGRETS. It took me three or four years before I finally heaved it out of my apartment window. How can you *not* have any regrets? It's impossible. No regrets? Bullshit. I don't believe anybody who tells me that.

Audiences like routine. They like habit. Nothing wild ever succeeds in television.

I don't socialize very much. Don't go to parties. I never get asked.

I had lung cancer about two years ago, and I was in the hospital after surgery with a staph infection. It was touch and go for a little bit. This nurse said to me, "Don't worry about it, Chuck. Bad grass never dies."

In the hospital, life didn't have any meaning whatsoever. I had just gone through a real bad divorce, I had cancer, I didn't have a book to write, nothing was happening. I just figured, here's what I'll do: When I get out, I'll get in the big green easy chair I have in my living room and I'll read all those books that I never had time to read. Books and me. Two years later, today, I'm married to a woman who's making me happier than I've ever been, they're making a movie out of my book, my other book is being published. So much has happened. It only proves that if you keep hanging in there, you just might be able to keep going on and on and on.

The glass is half full. It used to be half empty.

No matter what, I would have ended up writing. That's what I was meant to do. I hate to think that, because writing is an atrocious way to spend your time. It really is. It's boring and it's repetitious and it's just terrible. It's awful.

I'm trying to think of the next book I'll write.

One day you wake up and you're old as shit.

Living by the ocean is pretty depressing if you're living by yourself.

The Gong Show was the greatest scam of all time. It was simple: We wanted to do a talent show. There weren't any venues for acts back then. We were gonna have a show of new, fresh, good acts. But we couldn't find any; they were all lousy. So rather than throw away the idea, I said, "Let's reverse it. Let's do *lousy* acts." Now, is that a scam? I'm telling you.

I haven't watched *American Idol*. It doesn't interest me.

I'm cynical. People by and large disappoint me. Events disappoint me. And so there's a lot of cynicism in my bones.

Love comes later.

Tough love? That's bullshit. You love your kid and you keep on loving your kid. You take your kid back no matter what, and you keep on taking your kid back. Once, twice, a hundred times. The tough-love philosophy tells you to give your kid a million bucks and say, Don't come home until you're clean. Well, I did that. I gave my daughter a million bucks. She never got clean, and she never came home. She died.

I'm amazed how life can take something away from you so fast and then give it right back.

To me, dinner with four or five or six friends is living like a bunny rabbit. I tell ya, it's the best.

My circle of good friends has diminished over the years. I don't know if I have five friends in L.A. In New York, maybe ten. Over the years, for one reason or another . . . I don't know what knocks them off. I have this imaginary baseball field, and all the people I can't stand anymore I relegate to left field. I always say, "Oh, I stuck him out in left field years ago." Well, left field is jammed. I don't know what the cause of that is. Times change, you change.

Regrets, I've had a couple thousand.

INTERVIEWED BY TOM JUNOD // Photograph by Michael Lewis

bio

BORN: Philadelphia, Pennsylvania
June 3, 1929

> Barris was executive producer of *The Gong Show*, *The Newlywed Game*, and *The Dating Game*.

> Also a songwriter, he co-composed the hit "Palisades Park" for singer Freddy Cannon in 1962.
> Barris's first wife, Lyn Levy, was the daughter of one of the founders of CBS. Because Barris was working for NBC at the time of their marriage, Lyn's family disinherited her.
> In 1980, Barris starred as himself in *The Gong Show Movie*.
> *Confessions of a Dangerous Mind,* his "unauthorized biography," was published in 1984 and made into a movie in 2002.

Richard Branson

If you're embarking around the world in a hot-air balloon, don't forget the toilet paper. Once, we had to wait for incoming faxes.

My interest in life comes from setting myself huge, apparently unachievable challenges and trying to rise above them.

Once we get comfortable as a company, I like to push the boat out again. My wife keeps saying, "Why? Why? You're fifty. Take it easy. Let's enjoy it." But I'm in a fairly unique position. Yesterday, the first of nine hundred new trains arrived in the UK and went into service. We are going to transform Britain's rail system from the worst in the world to the best. If you can do a few things like that, when the body gives out, you can say you've lived a good life. If I put all my money in the bank and drink myself to death in the Caribbean, I just think that would be a waste of the fantastic position I've found myself in.

Sex is as satisfying at fifty as it is at twenty. But that first groping sex at fifteen or sixteen? Nothing beats that.

When hiring somebody, I never ask to see a curriculum vitae. I feel that since I didn't have one myself, it would be a bit presumptuous to ask to see anyone else's.

I'll be the first one to make a fool of myself in any way if I think it'll help the party.

The only thing I hate is cigarettes the day after.

What do I love most about my wife? Her children. She's not likely to like that one, eh?

The best advice I got from my dad? Wear a condom.

If you look for the best in your employees, they'll flourish. If you criticize or look for the worst, they'll shrivel up. We all need lots of watering.

bio

BORN: Surrey, England
July 18, 1950

> Branson is the founder of Virgin Records, the label that signed The Sex Pistols, The Rolling Stones, Steve Winwood, and Janet Jackson, among other music legends.
> He expanded the brand to include the Virgin Megastore, Virgin Atlantic Airways, Virgin Mobile, and Virgin Cola.
> In 1987, Branson's *Virgin Atlantic Flyer*, the largest hot air ballon ever built, was the first to cross the Atlantic Ocean, reaching speeds in excess of 130 mph.
> Branson was honored with the knighthood in 1999.

Hire people who will treat the switchboard operator as friendly as they'll treat the managing director.

When I graduated from Stowe, a big public school, my headmaster's parting words to me were: "Congratulations, Branson. I predict you will either go to prison or become a millionaire."

If you have a record company, don't put out crap. Sign bands that all of the staff believe in so that they'll work day and night to make them successful.

There was a lot to learn about starting Virgin Atlantic, so I asked Sir Freddie Laker whether he could help me. He gave me advice and then said, "Another thing, Richard, is the stress. I'm not kidding, you should have regular medical checkups." He said, "You need to go to the doctor and ask him to stick his finger up your bum. He'll be able to tell you what's what." Later, as Freddie was leaving, he turned to me and shouted, "One last word of advice, Richard: When you're bent over and the doctor's got his finger up your bum, make sure that he hasn't got both his hands on your shoulders!"

Create the best. The best hotels and clubs and airlines never go bankrupt. The best always succeeds.

Generally, when you meet a hero in life, you are disappointed. My impression of Nelson Mandela was enhanced.

Being circumcised at twenty-four is not a good idea, particularly if the night after the operation you find yourself watching Jane Fonda's erotic film *Barbarella*. Before I could stop myself, I had burst my stitches. Hearing my screaming, my first wife, Kristen, came running to see what the matter was. When she found out what happened, she was in stitches. I no longer was.

When taking a risk, make sure to protect the downside.

Bill Gates invited me to talk to thirty or forty chief executives from around the world. Just before I got up on stage, forms were handed out to everybody, and Gates said, "It's very important that all of us are tested in our lives. Richard's about to speak and I'd like you all to mark him 1 out of 10." Now, *that* intimidated me. I thought, Fuck, I thought I'd gotten out of school thirty-five years ago. I turned to the guy on my right—I think he was the head of Amazon—and said, "I'll give you a 10 if you give me a 10."

Try to avoid falling out with people. The world is a very small place.

Monogamy? What's that?

Over the years, the parties have got bigger and bigger, but the theme is the same: glorious irresponsibility for the night.

Get your priorities right.

INTERVIEWED BY CAL FUSSMAN // Photograph by John Midgley

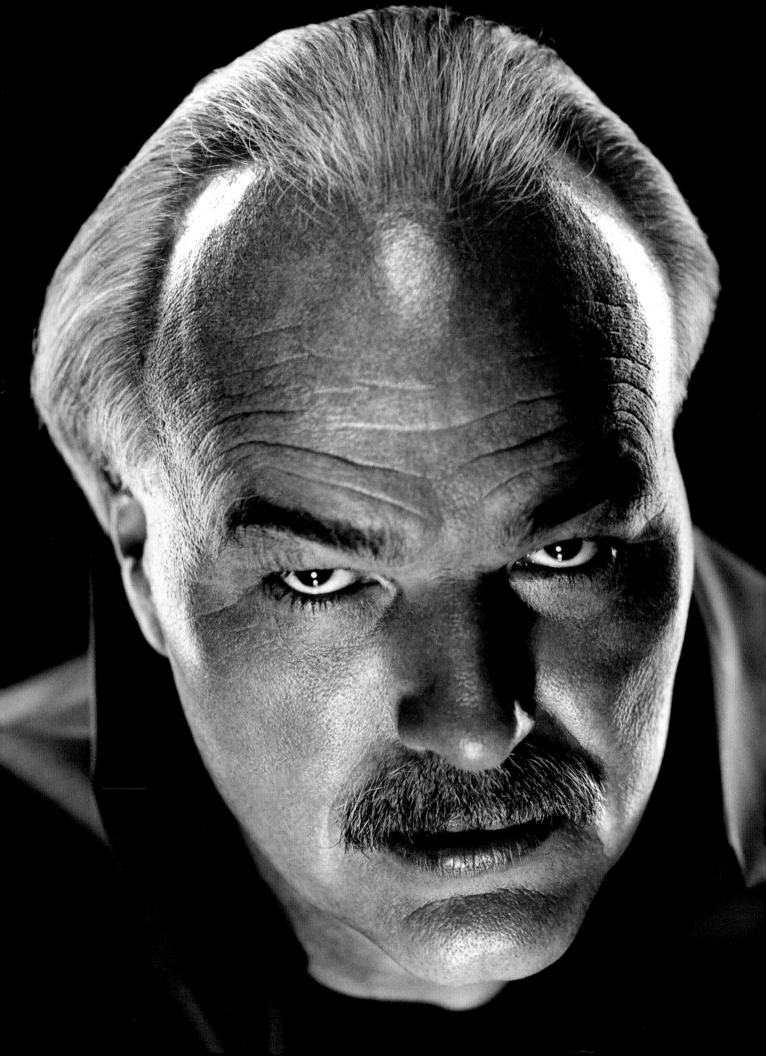

Conrad Dobler

You know you're getting to be old when you don't buy jujubes anymore. You get Gummy Bears instead because they're softer.

Positive thinking is a good attitude to have. But positive thinking without any skills is a load of crap.

Pride is hard to swallow, but it *will* go down.

I only bit one guy: Doug Sutherland of the Minnesota Vikings. He put his fingers through my face mask, and I don't think they were there to stroke my mustache. So I bite one finger in my life, and I don't even chew on it. The legend grew from there. It's almost like I'm worse than Jeffrey Dahmer.

If a dog can't go get your newspaper, why have him?

I was raised in a house that had only two bathrooms, and we had our grandparents living with us, too. Eleven of us in a house with two bathrooms. You learn to always check the toilet-paper roll before you use it to make sure there's paper there.

My father gave me a piece of advice: He said, "Never buy anything that eats while you sleep."

When guys come over to date my daughter, I'm going to tell them, "I want you to go out and have a very good time with my daughter. I want you to enjoy yourself and have her home on time. If you abuse her in any way, I'm going to kill your mother and father, cut your back open, pull out your spine, and leave you in a wheelchair so you can think about what you did for the rest of your life. Now, go out and have a good time!"

I like tits. If women had three, it would be even better.

One man's justice is another man's injustice—depends on whose pig is being poked. And that's the final analysis.

One game, I knocked the crap out of Merlin Olsen. If you wanted to see it on instant replay, you had to go to the kitchen because I knocked him so far out of the TV frame. After the game, he says, "One of these days, someone's going to break Dobler's neck, and I'm not going to send any flowers." What happens? He gets the $500,000 FTD commercial, and I don't get shit. He goes to the Pro Bowl fourteen times. He's in the Hall of Fame. He's probably got more money than God. When he was doing *Father Murphy* on NBC, he had a graveyard scene. One of the tombs said: CONRAD DOBLER. GONE, BUT NOT FORGIVEN. It's been twenty years since I played him, and I'm still on his fucking mind. *And I like that.*

I'll be damned if I'm going to pay someone $150 to unclog a toilet.

If it flies, floats, or fucks, rent it.

My definition of an oxymoron is a defensive lineman who gets a perfect score on the SAT.

Proper preparation prevents piss-poor performance.

The most amazing thing I've ever seen is the Holocaust Museum in Jerusalem. After we left, I couldn't speak for an hour. There's nothing you can say. For the life of me, I just don't understand it.

Pain is a state of mind.

Intimidation is a part of life. If it wasn't, the government wouldn't exist.

Throwing good money after bad doesn't work. At one point, I was $2.5 million in debt with no job—that puts you in a position that can get you to say, Maybe I should just put a gun to my head. But, you know something, that's just gnats on your ass when you compare it with parents who've got a ten-year-old with cancer.

Some people get vasectomies. I used to give 'em.

INTERVIEWED BY CAL FUSSMAN // Photograph by Len Irish

 **bio**

BORN: Chicago
October 1, 1950

> During his ten years in the NFL, Dobler kicked, punched, leg-whipped, and spat his way to three consecutive Pro Bowl selections and helped lead his team, then the St. Louis Cardinals, to four playoff appearances.

> Stopping at nothing to protect his quarterback, he was number one on the hit list of almost every defensive player in the NFL. In 1975, Dobler, Dan Dierdorf, and Tom Banks formed a Cardinals offensive line that tied the NFL record for allowing the fewest sacks in a season—eight.

> After he left the Cardinals, Dobler played with the New Orleans Saints for two seasons before finishing his career with the Buffalo Bills.

Larry Flynt

The two most misused words in the entire English vocabulary are *love* and *friendship*. A true friend would die for you, so when you start trying to count them on one hand, you don't need any fingers.

As to love, I'm reminded of when I was a child growing up with my grandparents in eastern Kentucky. One morning, I was looking out the window and seen my grandfather walking up the sidewalk. He goes into my grandmother's bedroom and hands her a flower and tells her her face looks like a beautiful May morning. To me, that's love.

I had to stand in a courtroom and listen to a judge say "twenty-five years in prison" before I realized that freedom of expression could never be taken for granted.

Nothing can make you more humble than pain.

Majority rule only works if you're also considering individual rights. Because you can't have five wolves and one sheep voting on what to have for supper.

Religion has caused more harm than any other idea since the beginning of time. There's nothing good I can say about it. People use it as a crutch.

When you're dead, you're dead.

These born-again experiences that you hear about all the time, they're nothing more than a chemical imbalance in the brain. These people need a little lithium and they'll be fine.

I subscribe to George Bernard Shaw on marriage. Love is blind; therefore, marriage is an institution for the blind.

Whether you've had an affair or not should not be a litmus test for entering the political arena. Most people want to keep skeletons in their closet. And they wind up getting in trouble as a result.

Bob Livingston told *The New York Times* that I was a bottom feeder. That's true. But when I got down there, look what I found.

bio

BORN: Magoffin County, Kentucky
November 1, 1942

> Flynt is the notorious founder of Larry Flynt Publications (LFP), which produces *Hustler* and over twenty other sex magazines. Annual turnover: around $100 million.
> Flynt made a brief run for president against Ronald Reagan in 1983.
> He has been involved in many legal battles regarding the regulation of pornography in the U.S.
> *The People vs. Larry Flynt* (1996) starred Woody Harrelson as Flynt, Courtney Love as his wife, Althea, and Edward Norton as Flynt's attorney, Alan Isaacman. Milos Forman directed, and Oliver Stone co-produced.

If the commitment is not there, it's time to walk away.

The conventional wisdom in Washington is that with Republicans it's money and with Democrats it's sex, but in actuality it's the complete opposite.

Hypocrisy is a detriment to progress. There's always a hidden agenda.

After the first million, money isn't important.

People in Hollywood are a greedy bunch of bastards who will use you up and drop you like a hot potato. I would rank politicians higher than I would the studio heads in this city.

If I like it, I buy it.

The biggest mistake I made was the mistake I made when I tried to figure out that my first mistake was really a mistake.

Women are smarter than men, they work harder than men, they're much more caring than men, they're much more committed.

All of our laws are made on morals; I concede that. It's not right to murder someone. But "family values" and morals today are a label for your sexual behavior, and that's what I find disturbing.

I always just hated the look of a standard wheelchair, and I figured, if you're going to be in one, why not be in a gold one?

It's not money, it's not politics—it's who controls the pussy that controls the world.

INTERVIEWED BY JOHN H. RICHARDSON // Photograph by Matthew Welch

Lauren Hutton

Supermodel
New York City

Courage? That's facing yourself.

Nature never does anything just for fun. It will throw fun in, but nothing is there *just* for fun.

Some people you talk to and the money they have is like a ticker tape coming out of their mouths.

When the termites swarm, it's a big pygmy delicacy. I was hanging out with this tribe in the interior of the Congo. This girl and I were tripping along one night in the dark jungle. She looked up at me and held out this swarming hand of bugs. She grabbed one, chewed it, looked at her hand, then looked at me. And so, being from Charleston and having good manners, I took it. Eating termites in the Congo is not like eating chocolate-covered ants. They're big guys. Two inches long, easy, and half an inch thick. They have big wings. Two pair. You use the wings as chopsticks. They have four legs, with grappling hooks on every foot that they use to hook on to wood. Sharp. You bite the head as he's coming at you, which stops him from breaking up your lips with those hooks. They're delicious—taste like Brazil nuts—though I didn't quite taste 'em until the seventh one because I was stoned on pygmy white lightning at the time. And thank you for letting me tell that story because it was a great time and I'm happy to remember it.

Travel is religious.

The closer we get to machines, the less manners we have.

Shakespeare is a reason to believe in aliens. Most authors have one idea per book. Shakespeare had two per sentence.

A Wrist-Rocket slingshot is one of the all-time great things to have.

Dads are real important to little girls. More than laps to sit on. It's a place to practice your sensuality. It's an animal that's not you. You and your mother are we. We are the same animal, come out of the same animal—which is an awesome connection. But this other rare fruit around, this rare bizarre thing, this mutant DNA—it's terribly exciting. Even before you know about sex. A *man*!

I'm always telling girls, "Listen to Granny: Don't show them the same old face over and over."

No model makes it if she has a big head.

The toughest tribe Bob and I ever lived with was the Karamojong. Northern Uganda. *Tough* boys. And the girls—*Jesus!* They fanged their upper and lower teeth. Filed 'em. No guide would go up to meet the Karamojong. But Bob somehow knew that they weren't going to kill us. And so we went.

We think clothes are more worthy than leaves, which is bullshit. There's some serious style out there in the bush.

Nature's main job over and over and over is to make a masterpiece.

I was a Playboy Bunny for three months. It was a good experience because it taught me pussy power.

I happen to have known very intimately a couple of octopi in my lifetime. They're extremely intelligent. Got me hot. I mean, I know it was wrong. And of course I never would have gotten too close. Because they might have gotten hurt worse than me, mentally.

The last of its kind is being killed every single day.

Styrofoam should be illegal.

Women will be fucked until half of all governments are made up of women.

You know how Reagan became president? For ten years on television, he opened the door to a GE refrigerator full of food.

I was thirteen when rock 'n' roll started. I was eighteen when birth control came over the counter. I was twenty-one when you could get acid that was real, not strychnine, post–Timothy Leary crap. I had a lucky birth date.

It's fun having good questions because in answering them you always learn about yourself, which is the most fascinating subject around.

INTERVIEWED BY CAL FUSSMAN // Photograph by Carlton Davis

bio

BORN: Charleston, South Carolina
November 17, 1944

> Birth name: Mary Laurence Hutton. Measurements on Hutton's first modeling information card: 33, 23, 34. Signature imperfection: the gap between her front teeth.

> In 1966, Hutton was discovered by legendary *Vogue* editor Diana Vreeland. She went on to appear on the cover of *Vogue* twenty-five times.

> She became the first million-dollar supermodel when she signed an exclusive deal with Revlon. She was also the original "Charlie Girl" in the long-running perfume ad.

> Film highlights include *Paper Lion* (1968), *The Gambler* (1974), and *American Gigolo* (1980).

> She is CEO of Lauren Hutton's Good Stuff, a makeup company.

Evel Knievel

You can fall many times in life, but you're never a failure as long as you try to get up.

Loving someone doesn't mean that you can love her for six days and then beat the crap out of her on the seventh.

Women are the root of all evil. I ought to know. I'm Evel.

This country has become a nation of the government, by the government, and for the government. Our politicians are destroying us. We need a revolt!

When you're mad at someone, it's probably best not to break his arm with a baseball bat.

Heaven is a place you can go and drink a lot of draft beer and it don't make you fat. You can cheat on your wife and she don't get mad. You get a beautiful female chauffeur with nice, hard tits—real ones. There are motorcycle jumps you never miss. You don't need a tee time.

Anybody can jump a motorcycle. The trouble begins when you try to land it.

The Internal Revenue Service is more ruthless than the Gestapo. Abolish the IRS! Stamp out organized crime!

I don't believe in hell. I don't believe in gods or Jesus Christ or sacred cows. I don't believe in that big, fat-assed Buddha. Show me one piece of Noah's ark. Show me one piece of the tablets that Moses was supposed to have brought down from the mountain. People need a crutch. They need to make up stories. I don't want to do that.

You can be famous for a lot of things. You can be a Nobel Prize winner. You can be the fattest guy in the world. You can be the guy with the smallest penis. Whatever it is, enjoy it. It don't last forever.

One day you're a hero, the next day you're gone.

People *say* they take responsibility for their own actions all the time, but that don't mean they really do.

I think that all of these so-called born-again Christians should ask their preachers why they don't hand out organ-donor cards. If you donated a kidney or a heart or an eye or whatever to your fellow man to keep him alive, you couldn't be closer to God than that.

You can't forbid children to do things that are available to them at every turn. God told Eve, "Don't give the apple to Adam," and look what happened. It's in our nature to want the things we see.

If God ever gives this world an enema, he'll stick the tube in the Lincoln Tunnel and he'll flush everybody in New York City clear across the Atlantic. And that would just be a start.

We must tax the churches. Freedom of religion is bullshit when it's tax-free.

You are the master of your own ship, pal. There are lots of people who fall into troubled waters and don't have the guts or the knowledge or the ability to make it to shore. They have nobody to blame but themselves.

I've done everything in the world I've ever wanted to do except kill somebody. There are a couple of guys I know who need shooting. They represent the rectums of humanity.

If you don't know about pain and trouble, you're in sad shape. They make you appreciate life.

Everything in moderation is okay, except Wild Turkey.

If a guy hasn't got any gamble in him, he isn't worth a crap.

INTERVIEWED BY MIKE SAGER // Photograph by Kurt Markus

bio

BORN: Butte, Montana
October 17, 1938

> Birth name: Robert Craig Knievel
> America's legendary daredevil started performing stunts in 1965. He rode through fire walls, jumped over live rattlesnakes and mountain lions, and cleared large obstacles on his motorcycle.

> Knievel was paid $1 million for his jump over 13 buses at Wembley Stadium in London, during which he crash-landed and broke his pelvis. He retired from stunt work in 1981 after suffering about 35 broken bones.
> In the '80s, Knievel had a second career as an artist. He sold thousands of limited edition prints of his mostly western and wildlife scenes.
> He has been a generous contributor to charities and currently promotes the work of the Make a Wish Foundation, an organization that arranges the fulfillment of the dreams of terminally ill children.

Suge Knight

Record executive
Los Angeles

Respect is everything.

When I was a kid in Compton, the other kids would say, "When I grow up, I want a Chevy." I would say, "I want a Porsche or a Rolls-Royce." I wanted something other than what I saw in the ghetto.

My first memory is of my father picking me up.

My father was a janitor who worked his way up to truck driver. He'd get home and be so tired, I would take his shoes off and he'd fall right asleep in front of the TV. No matter how hard he worked, he barely had enough money to buy himself an extra beer. He could have easily left the family like a lot of other fathers do. But he was loyal.

One thing I knew was that one day, I'd be paying a debt to the system. If you grow up in the ghetto and you're active, you're gonna get caught up.

I used to go to football practice in college and see how many teammates I could hurt.

Any time somebody comes to visit you in prison, that's good.

When we did the first hit record for Death Row, *The Chronic*, I treated it like it was a football team. It was double days in hell week. We had a quarterback, a center, offensive linemen; everybody had to work together, eat together, sleep together. And you heard that.

Who was the most talented rapper? Tupac. By far.

Solitary confinement is punishment. When you fuck up or they want to break you down, they put you in the hole. Your food is two colds and a hot. It's not enough to feed an eight-year-old.

What they don't tell you is how many people die in solitary confinement.

It seems like the more enemies you have in life, the better off you are. An enemy can't get close enough to you to do anything to you. He can't go to your house and turn around and steal from you. He can't come to you and borrow money. People who think everyone is their friend are leading a dangerous life.

I know the difference between something real and bullshit.

I enjoy myself with women. All my life, I've had a piece of a bitch.

You can't have it both ways on the death penalty. You can't say you believe in God and then go for an eye for an eye. I don't think you should kill a guy like McVeigh. Somebody who kills a lot of kids like he did, he just wants to get it over with. So what you do is you put him in prison for the rest of his life, and you put him on the main line, and you let the real convicts make him suffer.

The difference in playing basketball on the streets and in prison is that you don't call fouls in prison.

The worst part of prison was when my son would come to visit me. He'd ask, "Daddy, you coming home tonight?" When it was time to say goodbye, he didn't want to leave.

The key to running a business is to stay hands-on. If you really want to make something happen, you've got to lead by example. Even if you're the CEO, you've got to answer the phone.

Any time you do time and get out, just to hear a car run and smell gasoline is a blessing.

The only time you see women in prison, they're in police clothes. And they're *big* women.

Some guys have it real fucked up in prison, real hard. Some guys will be doing somebody's laundry. Some guys will be on their stomach with the pillow in their mouth. Some guys will be getting stabbed. If you're a man on the streets and you eat well, you'll eat well in prison. It just might be different food.

If me and Puffy Combs were on a deserted island together, it would be cool. I wouldn't have to tell him nothing. He would get the fish, cook the fish, get the firewood, start the fire.

My pit bulls and my rotts love me 'cause I wrassle with their asses. If they bite me, I'll bite 'em back.

bio

BORN: Compton, California
April 19, 1966

> Birth name: Marion Knight; Suge is short for his childhood nickname, "Sugar Bear."
> He is CEO of Death Row Records, which he co-founded with rapper Dr. Dre in 1991.
> Knight received a football scholarship to UNLV, where he also made the dean's list. After college, he briefly played for the Los Angeles Rams.
> In 1992, Knight was sentenced to nine years in prison for assaulting two rappers; he was later paroled. Another assault, caught on camera the same night as the shooting of Tupac Shakur, was a breach of that parole and resulted in another five-year term.

INTERVIEWED BY ROSS JOHNSON // **Photograph by Anders Overgaard**

Ted Williams

The bigger people are in life, the more big-league they are. That's been my experience. You meet less shits the higher up you go.

Some guys are just a little more inherently tough than the next guy. I think that's God-given genetics.

I wanted to play baseball. I don't know why, but I wanted to play. I had the opportunity, and I had desire. And talent. I heard some guy sayin', "Boy, that kid really looks good. He's quick. He's got good wrists." I said, "If that guy thinks I've got quick wrists now, wait'll the next time he sees me."

I don't envy Bill Clinton, but I am appreciative of him. He's done a lot of good things. And his wife—to me, she's the Joan of Arc of this country. Boy, I'll tell you, she's terrific. She has stuck with the guy. She's the greatest strength he's got.

Democrats are a strange breed. Although the greatest American we'll ever know in our lifetime is Roosevelt, no question about it. He wasn't my particular hero, but I give him tons of credit as president. But he could have been a little under-the-table, too, you know.

Ya gotta be ready for the fastball.

I decided I'd have a Cadillac. What the hell. I was kind of successful, and certainly it's a prestigious car. I got more tickets in that car. I figured, shit, they're just lookin' for Cadillacs so they can grab 'em for speeding.

I could have started smoking in the late twenties, but I didn't. I knew then that nicotine could attack every weakness in a person's body.

DiMaggio's the greatest player I ever saw.

The most fun I ever had in my life was hittin' a baseball. And the best sound I ever heard in my life was a ball hit with a bat. *Powww!*

I take two things into consideration if you're a guest: the city you're from and your exposure to baseball.

Pitchers are dumb. They don't play but once every four days. They're scratchin' their ass or pickin' their nose or somethin' the rest of the time. They're pitchin', most of 'em, because they can't do anything else.

In order to be called great, ya gotta have the circumstances surrounding ya.

I was a United States Marine pilot. It was the greatest experience of my life, and the greatest people in the world that I ever met were in the Marine Corps. The two things that I'm proudest of in my life, one is that I was a marine. The other thing is that I was lucky enough to play the game I loved.

Bob Feller's the greatest pitcher I ever saw.

The best? I don't really believe that. In my heart, I can't say and believe that I was any better than Lou Gehrig or Babe Ruth or Ty Cobb.

I'm not sure in my own mind that there's a supreme being. I don't have that much faith.

Rogers Hornsby was some kind of guy. Everybody thinks, Oh, Hornsby—what a mean bastard. He treated me like a son, couldn't have been nicer. And he gave me the greatest single piece of advice on hitting that I ever got: Wait for a good pitch to hit.

Sixty feet six inches. If it had been two feet either way, it would have changed the whole thing. I'm a real smart son of a bitch. I'm an old, dumb ballplayer and a real smart son of a bitch.

INTERVIEWED BY SCOTT RAAB // **Photograph by Brian Velenchenko**

bio

BORN: San Diego, California
August 30, 1918
DIED: Inverness, Florida, July 5, 2002

> Williams's nicknames included The Splendid Splinter, Teddy Ballgame, and The Kid.
> Nineteen seasons with the Boston Red Sox (1939 to 1942, 1946 to 1960) garnered Williams two MVPs, six American League batting championships, 521 home runs, a lifetime average of .344, and 17 All-Star Game appearances.
> After retiring from playing, he wrote a book called *The Science of Hitting* (1970). He also served as manager of the Washington Senators (1969 to 1971) and the Texas Rangers (1972).
> An avid fly fisherman, Williams was a frequent celebrity guest on ABC's *The American Sportsman*, which was created in the mid-1960s and lasted two decades.
> Upon his death, he was cryogenically frozen.

Gene Simmons

You can't argue with facts and figures. Either people want it, in which case they pay for it, or it's two guys sitting around at the Plaza having a discussion, which means *nothing*. I mean, *Titanic*. I wasn't crazy about the movie. But you know what? I'm gonna shut up, because the people have spoken. End of story!

My mother had a horrific life. At fourteen, she was in the Nazi concentration camps. Her sense about life now is, every day above ground is a good day. Just make yourself happy and don't hurt yourself. Make *yourself* happy.

Kiss is the number-one American band in gold-record sales. In the world, only the Beatles and the Stones are ahead of us. Every other band should be wiping my ass. The line forms over there to the left.

Prostitute yourself. As far as I'm concerned, that's even braver than waiting for the public to catch on.

I want more guys like Kurt Cobain and Jerry Garcia to become dried-up drug addicts and kill themselves. I totally defend all these rock stars' right to become heroin addicts and die. I want them all to die and get out of my way.

Up until the Asians started doing better in math, the Jews were the geniuses of the world! Einstein and almost every Nobel prize—forget about it, they're Jews! And that's because we don't play basketball. We *study*.

There's no message! Kiss is a Fourth of July fireworks show with a backbeat.

People say, "I want to get laid a lot and make lots of money." That's not the right order.

Dress British, think Yiddish.

A whore, in my estimation, has more credibility than a wife, and I'll tell you why. A wife is supposed to marry you for love. A whore is not there for love, she's there to service you. Now, the difference between them is a whore, before she does her work, will tell you exactly what it is. She'll tell you, "Blow job? This'll cost you seventy-five dollars. This is not love, and after I'm done I never want to see you again." *Full disclosure* is what they call it in court. A wife will tell you *shit*. A wife will tell you *nothing*. She's about to marry you. If you get divorced, she's going to take 50 percent of your gross pretax dollars and try to get more. Now, before you get married, if you dare bring up the notion, "By the way, let's just be completely honest with each other, what happens if we break up?" she will cry and tell you, "That's *so* unromantic." You know who's more credible? The whore.

"You can't buy love with money." Only a poor person says that.

Just because I'm Jack Nicholson in the insane asylum doesn't mean I'm one of them. It's just where I live. You know, it's . . . I'm Gene Simmons, and all the others are pretenders to the throne. I love that phrase. I'm gonna love reading that back.

When you go into a restaurant and you ask a chef to make you a spinach soufflé, do you really care whether he personally *likes* spinach soufflés? No! It's his job to make you the best spinach soufflé you've ever had, whether *he* likes it or not. I'd like to think I'm a chef. I'm gonna make you the best goddamn spinach soufflé you ever had, you'll pay me for it, and I'll be happy you did.

You shall not covet thy neighbor's wife? Well, how about if she goddamn covets *me*? What do you think about that?

I think Christians are wrong. They're wrong because you're not judged by your actions, you're judged by your beliefs, which is to say that if you're Hitler and right before you die, you say, "Jesus, I'm sorry," you get a better chance of going to heaven than the millions of people you killed.

The Koran is actually a beautiful book. Some of it has some good ideas. But these guys are out of their minds.

I think I know it all, relatively speaking.

My last meal? A Double Whopper and a Linzer tart.

INTERVIEW AND PHOTOGRAPH BY CHRIS BUCK

bio

> **BORN:** Haifa, Israel
> August 25, 1949

> Birth name: Chaim Witz. His mother, a Holocaust survivor, brought Gene to America when he was nine.

> The Demon, Simmons's fire-breathing, tongue-waggling, blood-drooling Kiss character, fronted the band that rocked the world with the manifesto "Rock and Roll All Nite."
> Simmons launched his own record label, Simmons Records, in the '80s.
> He co-produced and made a guest appearance in the film *Detroit Rock City* (1999).

Ike Turner

Musician
San Marcos, California

I'm pure with myself, man. I don't bullshit Ike. I bite the bullet. I don't lie to me.

You can feel when people are yessin' you. You can feel the real.

I always showed them what to do. I can go and record any girl you bring in here right now and you would swear to God she's coppin' off Tina—because there *is* no Tina. You hear *me* through Tina. I do it all. I do every bit of it. Every note that's played. When you saw Ike and Tina, every step came from me. All that shit came dead out of me.

You got to stand for somethin' or you'll fall for anything.

I know that people are stuck in cocaine, and I know that you feel it start off as fun, and then you wake up lookin' for it, and then you want out, because you see your life and you feel there's no way out. I say it like this: It's like you have glasses on and you can really see clear. So once, man, you put the stuff on it and it's a little brighter, but what happens is, when the stuff dies, now it's dull. You can never get it back clear unless you put some stuff on it. So every day you wake up, you put some stuff on it to clear it up, and you never can get it back clear. So you gotta go all the way to zero, where you can't see shit, and then you can find a light down there. There is a light there, but you have to really want it to get it.

I had to hit bottom. And when I hit bottom, it was like jail was the best thing ever happened to me.

People meet me and say, "Man, you're nothin' like what I thought you were. You're nothin' like that movie." But, man, that movie is not *me*. They had to have a villain. They assassinated my career with that damn movie, man.

Where's the Ray Charleses, the Sam Cookes, the Jackie Wilsons, the Louis Jordans? Where? It's no more. Black radio died.

BORN: Clarksdale, Mississippi
November 5, 1931

> A bandleader and record producer, Turner discovered, developed, and recorded legendary artists including Howlin' Wolf, Little Walter, Muddy Waters, and Little Milton.

> Most famously, he produced both Janis Joplin and Tina Turner. Ike was married to Turner for eighteen years; their relationship was notoriously volatile. See the film *What's Love Got to Do With It* (1993) for one interpretation.

> During Black History Month, Turner regularly goes to high schools to perform and jam with student musicians.

Kids took to the street with rap and hip-hop. "Shoot him. Kill him. The bitch this. The bitch that." This is what they had to do to sell records. So they did it. But the rest of this life that I got in me, man, I'm gonna use it to get black music back on the radio. Because there's very few of us left. Motown sold out—that's dead.

It make me happy to make you happy, but I'm not gonna make you happy by makin' me sad—and if I got to marry you because you want a husband, uh-uh. That's dead. I'll never get married again. That was number thirteen I just got a divorce from. Took a long time for me to learn, didn't it? I'm through, man. You can bet your bottom dollar.

What am I? I'm an organizer. Next, I'm a piano player.

I'm alive today and enjoying what the fuck I do.

To me, the onliest two people that ever had freedom in America is a white man and a black woman. They can do what the shit they wanna do. A black woman in Mississippi could slap the shit out of a white man—there ain't nothin' gonna happen to her. Rosa Parks, if she hadda been a black dude that done that, they woulda hung him on the highest tree. I'm just bein' real about it.

When you don't like whites, or you don't like blacks, well, you're just cheating your own self.

I call some people RadioShacks—if you got questions, we got answers. They got answers for every fuckin' thing.

One of the wrongs that I did in my life was that I fired this guy because he was too slow with them pedals, and come to find out ten or twelve years later it was Jimi Hendrix. You can't win 'em all.

If he have millions of dollars, I been there. If he's poor, eating out of the garbage can, I been there. If he have fifty women, I had that. If he lookin' for one, I been there, too. I've lived my life.

Don't do shit about me when I die. Let me rest.

Everything is a hole. When you're born, two holes—there's a hole at the head of your penis, and you come out of a hole. So you come out, and everything is about holes. When you eat? Hole. When you breathe, it's a hole. When you see, it's a hole. When you hear, it's a hole. And when you die, where you goin'? Right back *in* the hole. If you get too much money, you gonna be in a hole. If you don't get enough, you're definitely gonna be in a hole. So to me, the best thing to do is stop tryin' to stay outta the hole: Get in the hole and find out what's happenin' with the hole and try to control the hole. And then you can have the hole, because you understand the hole.

I know you heard what I said, but did you understand what I *mean*?

INTERVIEWED BY SCOTT RAAB // Photograph by Chris Buck

Ted

Williams

Baseball player
Hernando, Florida

The bigger people are in life, the more big-league they are. That's been my experience. You meet less shits the higher up you go.

Some guys are just a little more inherently tough than the next guy. I think that's God-given genetics.

I wanted to play baseball. I don't know why, but I wanted to play. I had the opportunity, and I had desire. And talent. I heard some guy sayin', "Boy, that kid really looks good. He's quick. He's got good wrists." I said, "If that guy thinks I've got quick wrists now, wait'll the next time he sees me."

I don't envy Bill Clinton, but I am appreciative of him. He's done a lot of good things. And his wife—to me, she's the Joan of Arc of this country. Boy, I'll tell you, she's terrific. She has stuck with the guy. She's the greatest strength he's got.

Democrats are a strange breed. Although the greatest American we'll ever know in our lifetime is Roosevelt, no question about it. He wasn't my particular hero, but I give him tons of credit as president. But he could have been a little under-the-table, too, you know.

Ya gotta be ready for the fastball.

I decided I'd have a Cadillac. What the hell. I was kind of successful, and certainly it's a prestigious car. I got more tickets in that car. I figured, shit, they're just lookin' for Cadillacs so they can grab 'em for speeding.

I could have started smoking in the late twenties, but I didn't. I knew then that nicotine could attack every weakness in a person's body.

DiMaggio's the greatest player I ever saw.

The most fun I ever had in my life was hittin' a baseball. And the best sound I ever heard in my life was a ball hit with a bat. *Powww!*

I take two things into consideration if you're a guest: the city you're from and your exposure to baseball.

Pitchers are dumb. They don't play but once every four days. They're scratchin' their ass or pickin' their nose or somethin' the rest of the time. They're pitchin', most of 'em, because they can't do anything else.

In order to be called great, ya gotta have the circumstances surrounding ya.

I was a United States Marine pilot. It was the greatest experience of my life, and the greatest people in the world that I ever met were in the Marine Corps. The two things that I'm proudest of in my life, one is that I was a marine. The other thing is that I was lucky enough to play the game I loved.

Bob Feller's the greatest pitcher I ever saw.

The best? I don't really believe that. In my heart, I can't say and believe that I was any better than Lou Gehrig or Babe Ruth or Ty Cobb.

I'm not sure in my own mind that there's a supreme being. I don't have that much faith.

Rogers Hornsby was some kind of guy. Everybody thinks, Oh, Hornsby—what a mean bastard. He treated me like a son, couldn't have been nicer. And he gave me the greatest single piece of advice on hitting that I ever got: Wait for a good pitch to hit.

Sixty feet six inches. If it had been two feet either way, it would have changed the whole thing. I'm a real smart son of a bitch. I'm an old, dumb ballplayer and a real smart son of a bitch.

INTERVIEWED BY SCOTT RAAB // Photograph by Brian Velenchenko

bio

BORN: San Diego, California
August 30, 1918
DIED: Inverness, Florida, July 5, 2002

> Williams's nicknames included The Splendid Splinter, Teddy Ballgame, and The Kid.
> Nineteen seasons with the Boston Red Sox (1939 to 1942, 1946 to 1960) garnered Williams two MVPs, six American League

batting championships, 521 home runs, a lifetime average of .344, and 17 All-Star Game appearances.
> After retiring from playing, he wrote a book called *The Science of Hitting* (1970). He also served as manager of the Washington Senators (1969 to 1971) and the Texas Rangers (1972).
> An avid fly fisherman, Williams was a frequent celebrity guest on ABC's *The American Sportsman*, which was created in the mid-1960s and lasted two decades.
> Upon his death, he was cryogenically frozen.

The Leaders

Red Auerbach

Bobby Bowden

Rudy Giuliani

Ted Kennedy

John McCain

Robert McNamara

Sumner Redstone

Jack Welch

John Wooden

Red Auerbach

Basketball coach
Washington, D.C.

If you're keeping score, win.

I was a coach who listened. I had guys when I was coaching who were in their thirties, like Cousy, Havlicek, Russell, all those guys. They were very bright. I've got to be stupid, as a coach, not to utilize their intelligence.

Power is ego.

You play as you practice.

You've got to avoid overcoaching. You've got to avoid talking too much. You've got to avoid showing players that you're the boss every time. You don't have to do that. They know you're in charge.

If you're comfortable in a situation, stick with it.

You got to be lucky. Like. for example, one time in the seventh game of a playoff, somebody took a shot—I think it was Nelson or Ramsey or Sam—and it hit the backboard, hit the rim, rolled around, went in, and made me a hell of a coach. You know what I mean?

God? I don't want to go into that.

You want an occasional beer, go ahead. But stay off the hard stuff.

What bugs me quite a bit is to have a coach whose team is twenty points ahead with three minutes to go, and he's up there coaching and moving and making all of those kinds of things [waves hands], and—why? Because he thinks he's on TV. The game is over. He should sit his ass down and relax.

For every hundred autographs you sign, the one you don't sign, you're a louse.

Eighty percent of the announcers who do color on TV are fired coaches. If they were such experts, why'd they get fired?

Black, white, or whatever, we didn't give a damn. If you could play, you could play, and that's the way we were.

Loyalty is a two-way street.

You know what bothers me? All these ballplayers, they all want to play for contenders. That's bullshit. You play where you're playing and do the best you can and let things work out. It's like coaches. When you get a good coach, whether it be a Phil Jackson or somebody else, what the hell does it take to have a ready-made ball club that's star-studded?

Grandchildren will wear you out.

There's no player today who compares to Bill Russell. As great as Shaq is, it would have been interesting to have Chamberlain knock bodies with him or Russell blocking all his shots. See? Oscar Robertson, Jerry West, John Havlicek, shoot! I mean, John Stockton is a hell of a player, but I don't take him ahead of Cousy.

There are ways to gain an edge. I'll give you an example: If you're playing against a fast-breaking team, you put new nets up so the ball won't go through quick. It hangs up. In kickball, you water the field the night before or you let the grass grow. In hockey, you make soft ice if you're playing against a fast team. In baseball, you raise or lower the pitcher's mound according to *your* pitcher, not their pitcher.

If they think we got an edge, we got an edge.

If you get up in the morning and you say, "Goddamn, I got to go to the office. I got to go to work. How can I get out of this?" and, I mean, you've got that kind of a feeling, you're not happy.

It's a great feeling to be the coach of the best team in the world.

If you don't feel like doing something, don't do it. My cardiologist told me that.

INTERVIEWED BY CHARLES P. PIERCE // Photograph by Nigel Parry

bio

BORN: Brooklyn, New York
September 20, 1917

> Head coach of the Boston Celtics from 1950 to 1966. Under Auerbach's leadership, the Celtics won eight straight NBA championships (1959–1966), a winning streak unmatched in basketball history.
> Auerbach was the first pro-basketball coach to win 1,000 games. He coached eleven Hall of Famers.
> After retiring from coaching, Auerbach became the Celtics's general manager. In 1980, he was named NBA Executive of the Year.

Bobby Bowden

I'm as happy now as I've ever been. I could've said that a week ago. And the week before that.

At this point, I don't want to see a problem unless it's big.

You got some guys who are mean, some guys who are sweet. The sweeter ones make better offensive linemen.

The good old days weren't so good when you were sitting in a dentist's chair.

If Steve Spurrier were coming over for dinner, what would I cook for him? Nothin'. I don't cook. I don't cook cereal. Not even cold cereal. I'm tellin' ya, I don't cook *nothin'*! I might take him out to a good restaurant, though.

I'm basically the same person I was at ten years old, just wiser. You get older and you get to sayin', "Do away with that. Do away with that. Do away with that. Do this; *this* is what's important." That's what you learn with age.

Happiness is not money and it's not fame and it's not power. Those are nice, but they only last a finger snap. Happiness is a good wife, a good family, and good health.

Courage is doing something you need to do that might get you hurt.

If you don't discipline your children, the sheriff's gonna.

Why does everyone make such a big deal about "wide right"? If you're gonna miss, you can't be anything *but* wide right or wide left. It's bound to be one of 'em.

When I coached at West Virginia and we began to integrate back in the sixties, white people used to come up to me and say, "How many black guys you got on the team?" I'd say, "I don't know. I don't count." They're all some mama's son to me.

bio

BORN: Birmingham, Alabama
November 8, 1929

> Head coach of the Florida State Seminoles, the most consistently successful college football program ever. Bowden is the only coach in the history of Division I-A football to compile 10 straight 10-win seasons. He holds the NCAA record with 11 consecutive bowl victories and 14 straight bowl trips without a loss.
> Among his many honors are National Coach of the Year (1979), Florida Sports Hall of Fame (1983), and ACC Coach of the Year (1993).
> Bowden and his son, Terry, the former head coach at Auburn University and 1993's Coach of the Year, are the first father-son duo to lead Division I-A programs, let alone coach them at the same time.

Heaven is nothing but good.

You ain't gonna get to the top unless you've got a little poise.

Ann was sixteen when I married her. I was nineteen. I'm not embarrassed to tell the story. You see, both Ann and I were taught you must be married before sex. We had been dating since she was thirteen or fourteen. You know how intimate you get. Well, we were so in love with each other, we couldn't control it. We needed to go get married.

I've always believed in second chances.

Is America a better place now than fifty years ago? Degree by degree by degree, I feel we have lost our morality. Our standard of living is higher, though.

Darkest day of my coaching career in forty-seven years was at my first head-coaching job at a major college—West Virginia. We played Pitt, the big rival. For those folks, that game is like Florida State–Florida or Auburn–Alabama. You go to coach at West Virginia and you want to make the fans like you, you beat Pitt. We go up there in 1970, and we get ahead, 35–8, at the half. I thought, Just go out there and don't make any mistakes and we got the game won. Well, we go back out and lose, 36–35. *Whooooooo!* I learned a lot from that loss to Pitt. I've never let it happen again. People get on me for running up the score. Don't care. I'll never sit on the ball again.

If somebody mistreats you, treat 'em good. That kills 'em.

Routine is imperative in football. Repetition, repetition, repetition. Until it becomes habit, habit, habit.

I take it for granted. I go home and the clothes are washed. Ann's always got the heat like we want it. She's a great cook. If something ever happened to my wife, what would I do?

My favorite song? Of all time? "New York, New York."

I look back and say, Why, I'll be doggone. Where did it go? I was just in college. How come I'm seventy-one?

INTERVIEWED BY CAL FUSSMAN // Photograph by Gerald Forster

Rudy Giuliani

Former mayor
New York City

The most important lesson my dad taught me was how to manage fear. Early on, he taught me that in a time of emergency, you've got to become deliberately calm. He used to say, "The more people are yelling and screaming around you, the calmer you should become. Become unnaturally calm. Somebody's got to be able to figure a way out of the jam. And you'll be able to do that."

Courage is managing fear to accomplish what you want to accomplish.

This is what defines a leader: Someone who has his own ideas. Someone who can see beyond today, into tomorrow and the next day. Someone who can see where we have to be. Someone who understands that *somebody* has to do that.

As a kid, I thought about becoming a priest. During my last year in high school, I had pretty much decided to go into the seminary. It wasn't like there was one moment that following summer when a girl passed and I knew that the seminary would not be a good idea. Actually, there were a *lot* of moments like that.

As a lawyer, I learned this rule: For every one hour in court, you want to put in four hours of preparation. You want to anticipate every question. Anticipate every answer. Write it all out. If you do that, nothing should ever happen in the courtroom that you won't know the answer to. And yet in every complex trial something happens that you didn't anticipate. Your answer to that will emerge from everything you've anticipated.

Instead of ignoring a problem, try to reduce it.

Winston Churchill is the person I'd most like to have met. I'd like to ask him about doubt. I'd like to ask him how much doubt he had about whether England could get through. What would happen if Germany had invaded? I would like to have spent hours with Churchill. I kind of *do* spend hours with him, reading about him. But you never know when you read about somebody. A lot of things have been written about me. Some of which are true. Some of which aren't true. I never know when I'm reading about somebody if I'm getting to know them or getting to know the person who's writing about them.

The person to negotiate with is the person who can deliver.

I changed my hairstyle at the end of last summer. It wasn't planned. It just happened. I used to comb it over. But one day, after showering, I combed it back and Judith said, "It really looks a lot better that way." I said, "It *does*?" She said, "Yeah, it looks great!" Nothing like a little positive reinforcement. I pushed it back for a few days and then got it cut that way. Feels good.

When I was six years old, my image of God was probably of a father figure. My image of God now is of a divine force that we can't describe because it's beyond our understanding. A plan that we don't know the full nature of, a plan that allows us through free will to make choices—some of which are good and some of which are bad. It's our job to make the best choices we can make.

The last thing I said to Father Judge at the World Trade Center was, "Please pray for us." And he said, "I always do." Then he smiled and we parted. I've seen the videotape of him in the area below the tower with a concerned look on his face. It was different from the last look that I saw him with. Something happened in the ten minutes between those two events. He must have had the same realization I had. Because when I first arrived there, I didn't realize how bad it was. When I finally got to the fire-department command post at the base of the north tower and looked up and saw a man jumping, that's when it clicked in my mind: This is beyond anything we've ever experienced.

I can't count out options. I've always operated this way. When I was running for reelection as mayor, they wanted me to promise I would serve out the full four years. I said, "I can't promise that. I can tell you that it's my intention. But I can't promise to do that. I don't know what's going to happen." I didn't know at the time that Senator Moynihan would resign. I knew I was going to be term-limited, and maybe in the last two years of my administration I'd want to do something else. Not that I had a thought in mind. But I never want to be in a position where I rule out doing something and then, all of a sudden, two or three years later, it makes sense to do it. Then you have to live with what you ruled out. So I created this rule for myself: Don't rule out options. Which, of course, then creates speculation that you're running for something…

INTERVIEWED BY CAL FUSSMAN // Photograph by Platon

bio

BORN: Brooklyn, New York
May 28, 1944

> Mayor of New York City, 1994 to 2001.
> Giuliani is widely hailed for his calm and effective leadership during the September 11 attacks on the World Trade Center. For this, he was named *Time* magazine's Person of the Year and was given an honorary knighthood.
> Giuliani often appeared on *The Late Show with David Letterman*, sometimes as a guest and sometimes in comedy segments; he also hosted an episode of *Saturday Night Live* in 1997.
> He is a lifelong Yankees fan.

Ted Kennedy

If I could have a meal with anybody, living or dead, who would it be with? My brothers who left too early. My sisters. My parents. I always associated the times when we were together—and there weren't that many times when we were all together—as the happiest times. There'd be magnificent conversation. It would be blueberry season, and my mother would ensure that we'd have blueberry muffins. We'd have blueberry pancakes. We'd have blueberry pie. We'd have blueberry *everything*.

There isn't a day that goes by when I don't think about my brothers.

My father would say, "Do the best you can. And then the hell with it." He always looked at the effort grade rather than the final grade.

When I was seven, I had the honor of receiving my first holy communion from the pope when my family went to Rome for his coronation. There were seven seats allocated to the United States and each of the major world powers. My parents arrived at St. Peter's with nine children. So there were eleven of us in seven seats. I, being the youngest, was squeezed to the far end of a very small bench. I remember one of the central thoughts I had during the whole ceremony: being squeezed in but still not being separated. That had a lot of significance to me over the course of my life.

When I was a boy, I used to look up at the sky at night and stare at the stars. I thought they were little pinpricks in a big covering and that the bright light that came through was really heaven on the other side.

My mother was the safe harbor for our family. The gift of faith came from her.

There are too many people being left behind and left out.

I like to have two dogs in my office. Splash, here, is wonderful company. He's got a great personality. He's been known to bark when people speak too loudly or for too long. Some have asked that we make him a permanent member of our Democratic party caucus so that speeches will be shorter.

My favorite restaurant? Dunkin' Donuts. Uh-oh. Better not say that. Besides, that's not a restaurant. Make it…Legal Sea Foods.

You must be prepared for good luck.

If you make a mistake: Recognize it, learn from it, and move on.

A good marriage is loving someone in a lot of different circumstances. Respect for them and their views and ideas and the life that they're leading with you. Shared values and interests. A good sense of humor. And a little volatility along the way.

bio

BORN: Brookline, Massachusetts
February 22, 1932

> Edward "Ted" Kennedy is the youngest child of Joseph P. Kennedy.
> A Democratic senator since 1962, he is known for his well-researched, clearly defined social-welfare legislation.
> He was first elected to finish the term of his brother, John F. Kennedy, after JFK became president.
> He ran for president in 1980 but was defeated for the Democratic nomination by incumbent Jimmy Carter.

I said that I *knew* the first time I set eyes on Vicki. But then she brought out a picture. She had worked in my office as an intern years before I thought I saw her for the first time. So it wasn't really love at first sight. We still have that picture. It says: "To Vicki, Thanks for your work." And it's signed *Ted Kennedy*.

Having a child with cancer reaches to the very depths of your soul. Particularly because there is so little you can do, yet certainly more that you can do now than when Teddy had it. We were fortunate to have access to good health care. Secondly, fortunate to have health insurance. Many of the parents I met at the hospital had children who were taking a similar treatment. That treatment was to last for two years. Some parents sold their houses to pay for it. Some could only afford twelve or fourteen months of the treatment. They were asking the doctors: "What percent does that reduce my child's chances of being able to survive?" So, you ask me why I'm for health care. I didn't need a reason before, but that's a reason I'll never forget.

I'm continually fascinated by those who make a big difference in life.

When you're older, faith is a very powerful factor and force in helping you look for the hopeful aspects of life. It gives you a sense of purpose and resolution. It's a matter of great solace and strength.

There were nine Kennedys. Thirty-two in the next generation. And sixty-two in the next generation. Forty-four of those sixty-two are aged thirteen or younger. I'm very blessed. I took forty-two of them camping last summer for two days. We had a great time, but, well, what's the best way to say this? I'm not sure when we're going on the next camping trip.…

INTERVIEWED BY CAL FUSSMAN // **Photograph by Gerald Forster**

John McCain

U.S. Senator,
Arizona
Washington, D.C.

Politics is an extremely rough game.

In prison, my own vulnerabilities were made clear to me. My strengths as well as my weaknesses were made clear to me.

Seize the moment and be happy.

I have to choose my issues and priorities very carefully. Because even though I now have a dramatically increased influence, that influence is not unlimited and could be squandered.

I'd like to be twenty-five again.

Twenty-nine, maybe.

I learned that John McCain was a good night out, basically. Because there is a lot of spectacle and a lot of entertainment there.

People who hold certain institutional positions should have your respect until they lose it. But the rest of us mortals have to earn it.

I think Elvis is still alive somewhere.

It's very important to lose gracefully. You know, no bitterness, no anger, no remorse—can't display that.

Loyalty is, with a large number of people in this town, directly driven by what benefit can accrue from it.

The Vietnamese are very gentle. The only people that are more gentle are the ones who've suffered even more, and those are the Khmer.

Everyone I've ever known who served in the Peace Corps or the military or Vista may not have liked it, but they sure felt that it was an enrichment to their lives, and the broadening and maturing they felt were very beneficial.

My life was charted out for me, and I resented that. Not consciously, but clearly subconsciously. You know, ever since I can remember, as a little boy: "He's going to the Naval Academy." It wasn't whether he *might*. The question was *when*.

I'm prone to mistakes.

Humor is very important. I learned that in prison. It's a great way of defusing tension. It's also a great way of deflecting anger. But when it's used wrong, as I used it wrong a couple of times, you hurt people. And that's just not acceptable. I've done it a couple of times, and I've always regretted it. And I can't explain to you why I did it.

Americans are waiting to be led.

I regret it when I'm in some small country and see that they've taken the worst of our culture rather than the best.

I think historians will look at Bill Clinton with puzzlement and make the following judgment: that it was a great waste.

Several people who have some fame have come into my office. No one has had the effect Muhammad Ali had. I've never seen anything like it.

I believe that Muhammad Ali did have religious objections.

You should allow young people to make their own decisions as to what they want to do with their lives. Hopefully, your beneficial influence over the years will motivate them to do the right thing.

I hope that my son, Jack, whether he becomes a military person or not, will conduct his life according to the traditions of our family.

I'm the guy that stood fifth from the bottom of his class. If my old company officer had contemplated that I would make a serious bid for the presidency of the United States, he would have probably had either me or himself committed.

I can see myself believing that eighteen years in the Senate is enough. If you can't accomplish what you want to accomplish in eighteen years, then you probably are not going to in six more years after that.

Time passes so quickly.

Celebrity is kind of fun, you know?

INTERVIEWED BY CHARLES P. PIERCE // Photograph by David Barry

bio

BORN: U.S. territory of the
Panama Canal Zone
August 29, 1939

> McCain served in the U.S. Navy from 1954 to 1981. He was shot down over North Vietnam in 1967 and held as a POW in Hanoi for 5 1/2 years. Although he was offered early release when his captors

learned that his father and grandfather were admirals, he chose to stay because he believed that leaving would be disloyal to the other prisoners.
> His military awards include the Silver Star, Bronze Star, Legion of Merit, Purple Heart, and the Distinguished Flying Cross.
> He has served as a Republican senator since 1987.
> McCain ran for president in 2000, picking up significant momentum before ultimately losing the nomination to George W. Bush.

Robert McNamara

My first memory is still very clear in my mind. It was November 11, 1918. I can even remember the street I lived on: 16 Clement Street in San Francisco. I can remember the streetcars coming down Geary on Armistice Day with people screaming on top of them. There weren't enough seats in the cars, so people climbed on top and were cheering, applauding. Joyous! Mostly because we'd just won World War I. But to many it was more than that because they believed we'd just won the War to End All Wars. That's what President Wilson called it.

I was on Guam in March of 1945 on temporary duty with the 20th Air Force. I was with General LeMay when we interrogated the B-29 crews that came back from a bombing mission. That night, that single night, we'd burned to death eighty thousand civilians in Tokyo. I've lived through a lot.

As president of Ford, I introduced the Falcon. That was one of my favorites. I also loved the Mustang.

One of the most serious days of my tenure as secretary of defense was Saturday, October 27, 1962, when we were trying to decide whether to attack Cuba or not because of the missiles there. Events were slipping out of control on both sides. We were *this* close to nuclear war and total disaster. I remember leaving the White House that night to go back to the Pentagon—I didn't go home for twelve days, lived in the Pentagon—it was a perfectly beautiful fall night, and I remember telling George Ball that I wasn't sure we'd ever see another Saturday night.

After JFK was shot, I went to meet the plane that brought his body back from Texas. Then I went home and either Jackie or Bobby called and asked me to come to the hospital where they were carrying out the autopsy. We took his body back to the White House at about 5:00 A.M. There was a big argument among his associates about where he should be buried. Some said, "He should be buried in Massachusetts—that was his home." I said, "He wasn't the president of Massachusetts. He was president of the United States. He ought to be buried in Washington." I went out to Arlington National Cemetery to find a place. It was a gray and rainy morning, and the cemetery was shrouded in a faint mist. I walked with the superintendent across the beautiful grounds studded with simple white tombstones. I stopped when we came to a spot just below the Custis-Lee Mansion. I could see the Lincoln Memorial in the distance. "This is the place," I said. I called Jackie and she came out to look at it. That's what she chose. Later in the day, I was introduced to a young park-service ranger who had escorted Kennedy on a visit to Arlington a few weeks earlier. I told him which spot I had chosen. "When President Kennedy was visiting a few weeks ago," the ranger said, "he stopped in that same spot. He looked out toward the monuments, and I heard him say that this was the most beautiful sight in Washington."

It's done. You can't bring JFK back to life. I don't think about who did it.

I was forty-four years old when I became secretary of defense. I wish I had the knowledge I do now back then.

Vietnam we saw as a function of the cold war. The CIA appraisal was, and Eisenhower's appraisal was, that the loss of Vietnam and Laos would trigger an extension of communist hegemony across much of southeast Asia. This would weaken the security of the West across the world. Therefore, it was necessary to prevent that. That's why we were in Vietnam. It was an incorrect appraisal.

There is no contradiction between a soft heart and a hard head.

I've gone to the Vietnam Memorial. It brings me a feeling of sadness. But it also brings a feeling of respect and honor for the people who served their nation.

As the ancient Greek dramatist Aeschylus wrote, "The reward of suffering is experience."

bio

BORN: San Francisco, California
June 9, 1916

HIGHLIGHTS:
> In 1943, McNamara became a captain in the Air Force and served in the UK, India, China, and the Pacific. He was promoted to lieutenant colonel before going on inactive duty in April 1946.
> In late 1960, McNamara became the first president of Ford Motor Company who was not a member of the Ford family.
> He served as the U.S. secretary of defense from 1961 to 1968 under both the Kennedy and Johnson administrations.
> He was president of the World Bank from 1969 to 1981.

INTERVIEWED BY CAL FUSSMAN // **Photograph by Chris Buck**

Sumner Redstone

There is no question you will ask that I will not answer.

You have to fight for the last penny. If you don't fight for the last penny, you might lose the last ten million.

I was born in a tenement. The bathroom was not in our apartment but down the hall. That stays with you.

I went to Boston Latin. It was run like a private school, and it had the best kids from all around. The competition was cruel. I was working day and night, without letup. I graduated first in my class. After Boston Latin, Harvard was like kindergarten.

Success is not built on success. It's built on failure. It's built on frustration. Sometimes it's built on catastrophe.

The only thing that counts is competence. Not race. Not gender. Competence.

I argued a very important tax case before the Supreme Court in the fifties. I came up with a whole new theory on net worth and won. As a result, people got out of prison all over. Not long afterward, I went to Las Vegas. The word had spread, and I ended up having dinner with Gus Greenbaum and his associates. They offered me anything to represent them, but I wasn't interested. A short time later, Greenbaum was found stabbed to death. Evidently, I made the right career decision.

It's fair for people to question how much a CEO is making. But they should question the companies that *fail*. In the companies that have a great management team, they should understand that it's important to compensate great executives.

Wall Street has a short memory.

If the company is pleasant, the wine gets better.

I got a chance to see a preview of *Star Wars*. After it was over, I walked across the street to a gas station and used a pay phone to buy twenty-five thousand shares of Twentieth Century Fox. That's not necessarily vision. I was a movie exhibitor, and I thought I could tell when a movie was going to take off. You can't always.

People don't watch technology; they watch what technology brings into their homes.

I never think about the fire. I don't have nightmares about it. I only think about it when somebody like you asks a question. Today, we all know what to do in a fire. There was no education back then. They used to have fire drills in school that taught you nothing. I made the classic mistake. I was in a room in Boston's Copley Plaza when I smelled smoke. I opened the door and the flames swept in. The fire shot up my legs. The pain was seething, yet I can remember standing in the middle of this room, surrounded by flames, thinking, What a way to die. I got to one window and it wouldn't open. Somehow I got to another window and climbed outside. I was kneeling on a tiny ledge barely big enough to put one foot on. I'm three stories up. If I jump, I'm dead. Flames were shooting out of the window, and I just crouched there, hanging on to the windowsill, with my fingers cupped and my right hand and arm in the fire. The heat and flames burned off my pajamas and peeled away my skin. My legs had been burned to the arteries, and my arm was charring. I hung out the window by my right arm for a long time. How long? Forever. Finally, a hook and ladder came, and a fireman climbed up, cradled me in his arms, and carried me to the ground. They say that people can't remember pain. Well, I felt nothing right after—the nerves were gone. But in order to cover the wounds, they needed to take skin off the rest of my body. Having to strip half of your body of skin and use it to cover the rest of your body is very painful. I can remember that pain. I remember it like yesterday.

I don't believe in letting history get in the way of the future.

A good hot dog is almost as good as a steak.

I wouldn't like to have anything written on my tombstone. I don't want a tombstone. I don't want to die.

I am not a tough guy. I'm a tough negotiator. I'm a tough competitor. But outside of that, I'm a patsy.

INTERVIEWED BY CAL FUSSMAN // Photograph by Sam Jones

bio

BORN: Boston, Massachusetts
May 27, 1923

> Birth name: Murray Rothstein
> Redstone has been CEO of Viacom since 1987. Under his leadership,

Viacom has become one of the world's largest entertainment and media companies. Its properties include CBS, MTV, Nickelodeon, Paramount Pictures, Simon & Schuster, Comedy Central, and Blockbuster Video.

> In 2004, he was ranked number 35 on *Forbes* magazine's list of the 100 richest people in the world.

Jack Welch

Growing up in Salem, Massachusetts, we would play ball in a playground called the Pit. No organizing. Now kids get organized, driven here, driven there. My grandchildren live a life of three o'clock hockey and four o'clock piano lessons. Our mothers just sent us out the door. When you were small, you were always the last one picked for the team and put out in right field. The years passed, and then *you* were putting guys in right field. You learned one thing as you got older: You picked the best players and you won.

I was a terrific athlete until I was about fifteen. Then I never got any better. But I don't look back. I don't linger on the facts that my curveball stopped curving and I was too slow. I instinctively react to what happens. I'm always tomorrow.

My father worked as a railroad conductor on the commuter line between Boston and Newburyport. What he taught me about working was the other side of management. He taught me that bosses played golf. He didn't know anything else about it.

If the Red Sox win, they may not become as interesting. A long-suffering guy like me, who hangs on every pitch . . . How can anyone be a Yankee fan anymore?

Hate bureaucracy.

Your job as a manager is to carry a watering can in one hand and fertilizer in the other. Pour it over the seeds and watch the seeds grow. Now, you're gonna get some weeds. So you gotta cut the damn things out to improve the garden.

There are more stiffs out there than you can imagine.

My son John must have been eight or nine when he was sitting on a school bus that stopped for a pickup. We were living in a small town at the time. A kid climbed on and went straight for him and took a swing. The fight broke up quickly, but John had no idea what was going on. That night at dinner he told us what happened, and I asked about the kid's last name. As soon as he said it, I knew. I had asked the kid's dad to leave GE. I felt terrible. Terrible! But I explained everything to John. It wasn't like the guy was being asked to leave immediately. It wasn't working out, and he was being given time to find a new job. I was not being cruel.

In fact, I've come to learn that the worst kind of manager is the one who practices false kindness. I tell people, You think you're a *nice* manager, that you're a *kind* manager? Well, guess what? You won't be there someday. You'll be promoted. Or you'll retire. And a new manager will come in and look at the employee and say, "Hey, you're not that good." And all of a sudden, this employee is now fifty-three or fifty-five, with many fewer options in life. And now you're gonna tell him, "Go home"? How is that kind? You're the *cruelest* kind of manager.

Nobody was ever surprised he was let go.

You've made a bad deal. The plant's blown up. Marriages don't work out. A variety of things don't work. Keep goin'!

Money, for me, disappeared as a driver in the eighties.

Grasso is getting $139.5 million. Tell me, what should it be? Hey, by certain Wall Street standards, over a thirty-five-year career, that's not a hell of a lot of money. All I know is, Grasso did a very good job in a tough environment.

bio

BORN: Salem, Massachusetts
November 19, 1935

> Welch was CEO of General Electric from 1981 to 2001. Under his leadership, GE's profits increased 600 percent.
> Welch was known for his informal approach, which allowed him to interact with employees and get involved in all aspects of business. He was also dubbed "Neutron Jack" for his propensity to fire employees who didn't perform.
> *Fortune* named Welch "Manager of the Century" in 1999.

Love the janitor.

If I could, I'd be Tiger Woods.

Myself, I had very few original ideas. But I always smelled an idea from somebody and then did something with it.

Money is great when you can give it out.

It's in the worst of times that things get fixed.

One of the tragic things about getting old—and there are many—is the hangovers. They don't let you hang like you could when you were twenty or thirty.

Fears diminish over time.

Every day I do something I love doing. I've always been happy, but this just feels like the happiest. I'm *crazy* in love with Suzy. It's two years now, and it gets better every day.

My kids are all very good to me. And I'm not easy to be good to. I'm a little wild. You know, I had that public divorce. My oldest daughter graduated with Suzy from Harvard Business School. So it's not so easy.

When you're comfortable in your own skin, you can do anything. You're not worried about what somebody else has or what you don't have. You like *you*. Not in a braggadocio way. You just like *you*.

INTERVIEWED BY CAL FUSSMAN // Photograph by Nigel Parry

John Wooden

They called me the India Rubber Man in high school because every time I went down on the court, I bounced right up. Now I've had my hip replaced, and my knees aren't any good. I'm old. I accept it. One of my great-granddaughters said, "Pa Pa, you drive like an old man." I said, "Well, honey, what am I?"

Discipline yourself and others won't need to.

If I were ever prosecuted for my religion, I truly hope there would be enough evidence to convict.

I'll never adjust to the loss of Nellie. We were married for fifty-three years. No man ever had a finer wife. Prior to her loss, I had some fear of death. Now I have no fear. I look forward to seeing her again.

Passion is momentary; love is enduring.

Be more concerned with your character than your reputation.

If I am through learning, I am through.

My father gave me a two-dollar bill for my grade-school graduation and said, "Hold on to this and you'll never be broke." I still have it. A lot of times, that's all I've had. But I've never been broke.

The most I made coaching was $32,500. Maybe I didn't have a million-dollar contract like Shaquille O'Neal, but he'll never know what it was like to get a good meal for twenty-five cents.

Don't let making a living prevent you from making a life.

I don't think I was a fine game coach. I'm trying to be honest. I think I was a good practice coach. I could tell you right now what we did at every practice I had at UCLA—every day, every minute. It's all on paper.

When my son was in high school, he wanted a car. I said, "You work hard in the summer and save up for half, and I'll pay the other half." So he saved up, and I came home one day and Nellie was distraught. Jim had given his money to a friend. I said to Jim, "Do you think you'll get it back?" He said, "Dad, what did you always teach me? He's my friend. Haven't I heard you say your greatest joy is doing something for someone with no thought of something in return?" Hearing your own words come back at you can make you smile. Later that year, his friend paid him back.

I don't like to be like the guy in church who coughs loudly just before putting money into the offering plate.

I learned more from Lewis Alcindor about man's inhumanity to man than from anybody else.

I had three rules for my players: No profanity. Don't criticize a teammate. Never be late.

I don't believe in praying to win.

What am I proudest of? After we'd won a championship, a reporter asked one of my players what kind of racial problems we had on the team. The player said, "You don't know our coach, do you?"

Coming off the floor after the NCAA semifinal win over Louisville in 1975, it just hit me: Time to go. It was an emotional thing. I can't explain it. I went to the dressing room, congratulated my players. I said, "I don't know how we'll do against Kentucky, but regardless of the outcome, I never had a team give me more pleasure. It's been a great year, and I'm proud of you. This will be the last team I'll ever coach."

Never let your emotions overrule your head.

Never say never.

INTERVIEWED BY CAL FUSSMAN // Photograph by Gerald Forster

bio

BORN: Martinsville, Indiana
October 14, 1910

> Wooden is best known for coaching the UCLA Bruins from 1948 to 1975. In the 27 years he led the team, the Bruins never had a losing season.

> Wooden's team compiled the longest winning streak in college basketball history: 88 straight games, including back-to-back 30–0 seasons.

> He is one of two individuals enshrined in the Basketball Hall of Fame as both a player and a coach. (The other is Lenny Wilkens.)

> Wooden was honored as the college basketball Coach of the Year six times. He was also named the *Sporting News* Sportsman of the Year (1970) and the *Sports Illustrated* Sportsman of the Year (1973).

The Visionaries

David Brown

Chuck Close

John Kenneth Galbraith

Philip Johnson

Arthur Miller

Roman Polanski

Phil Spector

J. Craig Venter

David Brown

Work yourself to death. It's the only way to live.

I've never loved a dumb woman. The brain, combined with moderate good looks, is an overwhelming aphrodisiac.

Exercise is pushing away from the table.

I didn't learn to drive until I was in my forties and I moved to California. When I started to drive, I took my friend Robert Evans out, and he said, "You drive the way I fuck."

It doesn't comfort me to know that with my passing there will be no pain. I don't want to leave the party.

Marriage to a woman more successful than you can work, provided you take pride in her achievements and are secure in your own. For years I was known as Helen Gurley Brown's husband, and, frankly, I loved it.

Good health is beautifully boring.

When you visit the Hayden Planetarium at the Museum of Natural History and you realize the enormity of the universe and the insignificance of Earth and all who live on it, it's hard to conceive of a god in our own image.

Never sleep with anyone who has more trouble or less money than you have.

Children can age an adult faster than ten years in prison. Parents can have the same effect on children.

Bad dreams are more likely the result of strong cheeses than suppressed guilt.

The most unlikely women are the most explosive lovers.

Bad news is rarely exaggerated, and first reports of disaster can always be trusted.

Here's how to cure hiccups: Plug your ears with your thumbs and then, with your forefingers, clamp your nostrils so you can't breathe. At that point, have someone pour vodka into your mouth. Take three or four gulps. Voilà.

A man's attitude toward money is indicative of his meanness or generosity of spirit.

If you're going after mass circulation, you must have mass appeal.

I once took Mae West to a restaurant. Nobody bothered her. When we left, there was a standing ovation. That's respect. That's love. It's overdone now.

Never be the first to arrive at a party or the last to go home, and never, ever be both.

If you're broke, you'll live forever. If you're rich, you'll die tomorrow. To confound the fates, live it up, but little by little.

Avoid stocks whose names begin with *Bio* or end in *-ics* or *-ix*.

Success is a man who has the love and trust of a woman, a job he likes, and an abiding sense of humor. Success is a man whose children love him and have made him proud of them. Success is a man who dies at home in his sleep after a good life.

Eat just enough to fill out facial wrinkles.

What do I love about Helen? Her infinite configurations. Like a cat. No expression, movement, or phrase is ever quite the same. She's loving and funny and infinitely caring and has a work ethic that is admirable. She has a great laugh. What I love about her is everything. Everything.

I was at a party in Charlottesville, Virginia, about ten years ago with Muhammad Ali. My wife was out there dancing. Everybody was dancing. Only the two of us were left at the table. Muhammad said, "Tell me, can you still get it up?" I said, "Yeah, not great, but from time to time, yes." He said, "Just curious." I was charmed by the moment.

The biggest tip I've ever given? 100 percent. I always keep my hand over the bill so that Helen can't see it. She says, "How can I submit this bill on my expense account with this tip!"

I get good tables.

After seventy, if you wake up without pains, you're dead.

INTERVIEWED BY CAL FUSSMAN // Photograph by Len Irish

bio

BORN: New York, New York
July 28, 1916

> A former reporter, magazine editor, and short story writer, Brown didn't begin his Hollywood career until 1953, when he took a job as a story editor at 20th Century-Fox.

> Brown and Richard Zanuck produced two of the most successful films of all time: *The Sting* (1973), which won an Oscar for Best Picture, and *Jaws* (1975), which created a new genre, the summer blockbuster.

> *Driving Miss Daisy* (1989) was Brown and Zanuck's last commercial success before they dissolved their partnership. Brown produced *Chocolat* (2000) on his own.

> He is married to Helen Gurly Brown, author of *Sex and the Single Girl* and editor of *Cosmopolitan*.

Chuck Close

Inspiration is highly overrated. If you sit around and wait for the clouds to part, it's not liable to ever happen. More often than not, work is salvation.

Virtually everything I've done has been a product of—or has been influenced by—my learning disabilities. I don't recognize faces, and I don't remember names, either. But I have almost perfect photographic memory for things that are two-dimensional.

The choice *not* to do something is almost always more interesting than the choice to do something.

I wasn't a good student, I wasn't an athlete, and I think that helped focus me early in my life. I distinguished myself by being more intensely engaged and more intensely focused because I knew if I blew this art thing, I'd be screwed.

Get yourself in trouble. If you get yourself in trouble, you don't have the answers. And if you don't have the answers, your solution will more likely be personal because no one else's solutions will seem appropriate. You'll have to come up with your own.

It's always wrong before it's right.

Being a critic is like being a meter maid. All you do is bring pain into people's lives.

I'll tell you an interesting thing that's happened to me since I was paralyzed twelve years ago. I'm six foot three, and when walking around, I very seldom got approached by anybody. But being in a wheelchair has made me more accessible. I have people coming up to me on the street now. One of the great pleasures in that is that accessibility has made it possible for people to engage me in a different way. It's very moving to hear someone say my work has had some meaning for them.

Painting is the frozen evidence of a performance.

If you're by nature an optimistic person, which I am, that puts you in a lot better position to be lucky.

BORN: Monroe, Washington
July 5, 1940

> Close is celebrated for his huge, photo-realistic portraits. He takes photographs of friends (and sometimes, himself) and then paints from the prints.
> The Art Institute of Chicago, the Cleveland Museum of Art, the Museum of Modern Art, the Philadelphia Museum of Art, and the Tate Gallery in London are just a few of the museums that house works by Close.
> In 1988, he suffered a spinal blood clot that rendered him a quadriplegic. He continued his painting career in a new, loose style, creating colorful oil paintings that contrast dramatically with his earlier black-and-white portraits.

It happened suddenly, a spontaneous event within my body. I just found myself all of a sudden paralyzed from the shoulders down. It's like a car accident, in a way. There's a sense of calm; time slows down. It's not scary in the way you imagine something like this is going to be scary.

I'd rather not have these particular rocks in my shoes.

After a few days in the hospital, I was thinking, Oh, gee—I was raised in a church, Protestant upbringing, which I'd rejected as an adult—I'm lying in the bed thinking, Hmmm, maybe I ought to pray. They always say there are no atheists in a foxhole, and I thought, Here I am in a pretty good-sized foxhole…and I thought, *Naahhh*. I wouldn't respect any God who would listen to me after I'd rejected him so vociferously.

If you're overwhelmed by the whole, break it down into pieces.

An event like this, a catastrophic illness or whatever, it doesn't happen just to you, it happens to everyone around you. I sit in a wheelchair, but I look out at the world and it is unchanged. It looks the same as it always did. But people who love me look at me and they see a loved one in a wheelchair.

I miss being alone. Being alone is not the same thing as loneliness.

My favorite painter of all time is Vermeer.

Nuance and subtlety are where it's at. It's those little adjustments. You get something 99 percent of the way there, but it's that last 1 percent that really makes a difference.

You don't have to have a dramatic story. It's all in the telling.

I really miss the subway.

When I was first in the hospital and things were really grim, someone said to me, "Oh, you'll be all right because you paint with your head and not with your hands." And at first that really pissed me off. I thought, Easy for *you* to say. But it was absolutely true. Once you know what art looks like, you're gonna find a way to make it again.

Quadriplegics envy paraplegics. You think, Man, they've got it made.

Painting's been dead several times in my career already. And that's always the best time to start painting.

I didn't get into art for therapy. I go to therapy for therapy.

INTERVIEWED BY ANDY WARD // Image ("Self-Portait, 2001") by Chuck Close

John Kenneth Galbraith

Economist, ambassador, professor
Cambridge, Massachusetts

A good rule of conversation is never answer a foolish question.

Giving an opinion that people don't want to hear can work both ways. If it's a person you like, it can be very hard. If it's a person for whom you have a major distaste, it can be extremely enjoyable.

My mother died when I was very young, and my father was the dominant force in the family. In southern Ontario, he would have been called a political boss. In good Galbraith fashion, he took his eminence for granted. The most important lesson I received from him was that the Galbraiths had a natural commitment to political adventure.

For any sensible person, money is two things: a major liberating force and a great convenience. It's devastating to those who have in mind nothing else.

Modesty is an overrated virtue.

One of the characteristic features of John F. Kennedy was his wonderful commitment to the truth. We had breakfast together on the day I left to be ambassador to India in 1961. *The New York Times* was on the table and there was a story on the front page about the new ambassador to India. Kennedy pointed to it and said, "What did you think of that story?" which, needless to say, I had read. It wasn't unfavorable. I said I liked it all right but I didn't see why they had to call me arrogant. Kennedy said, "I don't see why not. Everybody else does."

I have no capacity to cook. It's a field of ignorance which I have carefully cultivated.

Franklin D. Roosevelt was good on great issues or small. A great war. A great depression. He presided over both. No question about it—he's the person who most impressed me. In my life, he had no close competitor.

I met Winston Churchill once. I went to a gathering that he assembled one night for a discussion on European union. I was principally impressed by the way his wife grabbed his arm every time he reached for another drink.

I've always thought that true good sense requires one to see and comment upon the ridiculous.

Is it good to have friends whom you don't agree with? Temporarily. But it has always been my purpose to get them to change their minds.

I have managed most of my life to exclude religious speculation from my mode of thought. I've found that, on the whole, it adds very little to economics.

I've long been an admirer of Adam Smith, who's greatly praised by conservatives—who unfortunately have never read him. They would be shocked to find some of the things Smith advocates.

Strong government, to some extent, is in response to huge problems.

In richer countries such as ours, I want to see everybody assured of a basic income.

Kennedy sent me to Vietnam in 1961, and I concluded from that visit that this was a hopeless enterprise. The jungle was something with which we could not contend.

If I had to pick out perhaps the greatest achievement that I've seen in all my years, it is in the diminishing role of race and discrimination. We have made greater progress there than I ever anticipated.

A shield against nuclear weapons is foolish. It owes much to the fact that the people advocating it are the people who would be benefiting from the effort.

How much money should a man carry in his wallet when he goes out of the house? I never thought of that.

INTERVIEWED BY CAL FUSSMAN // Photograph by Ken Schles

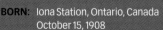
bio

BORN: Iona Station, Ontario, Canada
October 15, 1908

> During World War II, Galbraith served as deputy head of the Office of Price Administration.

> He became an economics professor at Harvard University in 1949, and still teaches there today.
> In 1958, he wrote *The Affluent Society*, a bestseller that has become a classic.
> President Kennedy appointed Galbraith the U.S. ambassador to India, where he served from 1961 to 1963.

Philip Johnson

Don't build a glass house if you're worried about saving money on heating.

I used to think that each phase of life was the end. But now that my view on life is more or less fixed, I believe that change is a great thing. In fact, it's the only real absolute in the world.

Sex isn't of much interest to me anymore, except inasmuch as you enjoy it in a beautiful room better than you do in a dull room. Sex is best in a cocoon. You have to feel wombish.

If architects weren't arrogant, they wouldn't be architects. I don't know a modest good architect.

Chain link is hardly a humble material, but corrugated tin doesn't mean anything to me.

I don't do a damn thing I don't want to. I wouldn't build a building if it wasn't of interest to me as a potential work of art. Why should I?

You're going to change the world? Well, go ahead and try. You'll give it up at a certain point and change yourself instead.

Pick very few objects and place them exactly.

Faith? Haven't any. I'm not a nihilist or a relativist. I don't believe in anything but change. I'm a Heraclitean—you can't step in the same river twice.

I'm not interested in politics, and I'm no good at it. You make mistakes.

Walk every day.

I got everything from someone. Nobody can be original. As Mies van der Rohe said, "I don't want to be original. I want to be good."

bio

BORN: Cleveland, Ohio
July 8, 1906

> An architect known for his unconventional designs, Johnson promoted the International Style, a school characterized by modern materials like glass and steel that emphasized function and structure over ornamental decoration.
> Johnson created some of the movement's major monuments, including the Seagram Building (in collaboration with Mies van der Rohe) and his own famed Glass House (1949).
> Other prominent Johnson-designed landmarks across the nation include the twin trapezoid-shaped Pennzoil Place in Houston, the 51-story IDS Center in Minneapolis, and the New York State Theater at Lincoln Center.
> In 1979, he won the first Pritzker Architecture Prize for lifetime achievement and the Gold Medal of the American Institute of Architects, the highest honor of his profession.
> He once described architecture as "the art of how to waste space."

I don't think there's any *why* about art. It's an end in itself.

I love money. I could make more beautiful objects if I had more money. But if you think about it too much, then it doesn't help your art.

How does an artist know when the line that he just painted is good or not good? That's the catch. De Kooning was the greatest of my contemporaries in art, and he knew when he'd done a good line. When he didn't, he threw it away. I wish I'd thrown away some of mine. You get involved and say, Well, maybe I can save this building if I do this or do that. Throw it away!

A lot of intellectuals are interested in words. Words annoy me.

Everybody should design their own home. I'm against architects designing homes. How do I know that you want to live in a picture-window Colonial? It's silly, but you might want to. Who am I to say?

Americans like to build on the road. I never could understand it.

Architecture is the arrangement of space for excitement.

Storms in this house are horrendous but thrilling. Glass shatters. Danger is one of the greatest things to use in architecture.

Comfort is not one of my interests. You can feel comfortable in any environment that's beautiful.

A room is only as good as you feel when you're in it.

If I could build one building in my life, I want to build a building that people feel in the stomach—you can call it comfort, beauty, excitement, guts, tears....There are many ways to describe the reaction to architecture, but tears are as good as any.

Put everything away and don't open the closet.

INTERVIEWED BY JOHN H. RICHARDSON // Photograph by Guzman

Arthur Miller

You have to learn how to duck, because they're gonna throw it at you.

Sex is the most compressed set of circumstances that we've got. Everything is in that collision.

What I'm doing is helping reality out. To complete itself. I'm giving it a hand. But there's some piece of reality that is a reported reality that it hangs on. It does hang on it.

When I was in Nevada, I lived about sixty miles out of Reno. There was a guy who had this house on stilts. In the desert. And that was a very curious thing, looking at this house raised up about ten feet above the ground. I wondered, Was he waiting for a flood? Well, it turned out he had a hole in the ground under that house, and there was a silver mine down at the bottom of this hole. He would periodically go down and dig himself out some silver. That was his bank. And I think that's like a writer. He's living on top of that hole. He goes down there and sees if he can chop out some silver.

There's such a variety of cultures in this country, we can be misled only up to a certain point. As soon as we start marching in step, somebody loses a beat somewhere.

I've always done things physical. When I was about six, I made a go-cart. You couldn't steer it and you'd be doing thirty miles an hour down the street, but I remember telling my brother, "Pretty good for my own making." He always used to kid me about that sentence.

I knew playwrights, young guys my age, who were simply not prepared to face the fact that their plays weren't any good. Mine weren't. I thought, Either I do this right or I'm gonna get out of it. I'm not gonna spend the rest of my life being a fool.

Sex is always trouble. That's part of why it's so pleasurable—because for a moment the cloud lifts and then descends again.

I don't believe in the afterlife. I don't believe there is a God. The whole thing is accidental.

Some people should never get married. Not everyone has that combination of dependency. You're leaning on somebody, and the desire to support somebody else, it just doesn't exist in some people.

I could write about failure only because I could deal with it. Most of my work before *Death of a Salesman*, 98 percent of it was a failure. By the time Willy Loman came along, I knew how he felt.

Whenever I hear somebody's in touch with God, I look for the exit.

The only thing that I am reasonably sure of is that anybody who's got an ideology has stopped thinking.

When plays were written in verse, by the very nature of the language it tended toward what I call prophecy. The energy of springing out of the dead level of contemporary reality. And we don't write that way much anymore, so something else has to enter—this spirit of coming disaster or coming happiness or something coming.

I believe in work. If somebody doesn't create something, however small it may be, he gets sick. An awful lot of people feel that they're treading water—that if they vanished in smoke, it wouldn't mean anything at all in this world. And that's a despairing and destructive feeling. It'll kill you.

The more sex the better. It may be a good thing to get it out in the open. You turn on the television now and they're screwing on the television. That's part of life. Why hide it in a basement someplace and get a lot of gangsters to distribute it?

Politicians are us, which is very dangerous. If they weren't us, it would be a lot better.

We have never, in my opinion, met up with this kind of an administration, which is extremely intelligent and has terrific control over the political life of the country. They are representing the rich people in a way that I didn't think was so blatantly possible. It's almost sociopathic. As though, Okay, if you can make it, you're one of us; if you can't make it, too bad, Jack. Some of the monkeys fall off the tree.

To write any kind of imaginary work, you gotta fall on your sword. You gotta be ready to be blasted out of existence. Lots of times, the blood is on the floor.

INTERVIEWED BY JOHN H. RICHARDSON // **Photograph by Inge Morath**

bio

BORN: New York, New York
October 17, 1915

> One of the leading playwrights of his generation, Miller has also published novels, short stories, and an autobiography, *Timebends* (1987).
> His most famous work, *Death of a Salesman* (1949), won both a Pulitzer Prize and a Drama Critics Circle Award.

> He wrote the screenplay for the film *Misfits* (1961) for his second wife, Marilyn Monroe; it was based on an *Esquire* short story published in 1957.
> Miller was elected to the National Institute of Arts and Letters, which awarded him a gold medal.
> In 1986, he was one of 15 writers and scientists invited to the Soviet Union to discuss politics with Mikhail Gorbachev.

Roman Polanski

I like shadows in the movies. I don't like them in life.

Memory doesn't last. When Kosovo started, they had already forgotten about Bosnia, let alone World War II. I remember after the war was over and my father returned from the concentration camp. He said, "You'll see—fifty years from now, people will have forgot all about it."

After Sharon's death, I definitely had a strong desire to give up. Your next question will be, What prevented me? But I can't answer it. I just survived. I was simply born this way. My father survived the concentration camp. I've been asked, Why did he survive? Well, I don't know. He wanted probably more than the others to survive. It can be anything. It can be the desire for revenge. It can be a longing to see your loved ones. Truly I don't know, and I never asked myself the question.

I think you should not ask yourself too many questions. It's the centipede syndrome, you know? The centipede was asked which foot he puts after which, and he couldn't walk anymore.

Work has always sustained me.

Sex is not a pastime. It's a force, it's a drive. It changes your way of thinking.

Kids just accept reality as it is, because they have no way of comparing it with anything else. I'm much more sensitive now to all this, having a child that goes through all these stages that I went through. She's now six: That's the age I was when the Germans walked into Poland. She's five: That's the age when my parents took me for the last holiday in the country. You see? She's seven: That's when I was running in and out of the ghetto through the hole in the barbed wire. I see it through her eyes, and it's only now that I realize that I was in harm's way. But at the time when I was a kid, no. The only tragic thing was the separation from my parents. *This* was something that made me cry, not that the food was bad, not that I had lice, not that there were fleas in the bed, not that there were bedbugs. And I think, you know, how tragic it would be for my daughter to go through that.

Movies always cost more than you have anticipated.

I think the Pill altered female thinking. When you think that millions of women were taking daily hormones, you cannot deny that it must have changed their personalities. I truly don't think that feminism would reach such absurd proportions if there were no Pill. It must have had an effect.

I don't think that Hollywood people like making movies. They like making deals.

After the party, you either clean up the mess or move the apartment. In general, I clean up.

There was no plot against me. There was no setup. It was all my fault. I think that my wrongdoing was much greater than Bill Clinton's.

Pleasure is a carrot. And a stick.

Films are films, life is life.

Never pull a hair from Faye Dunaway's head. Pull it from somebody else's head.

I'm not a masochist, but I always take a cold shower in the morning. It's a great beginning of the day, because nothing can be worse afterward.

INTERVIEWED BY JOHN H. RICHARDSON // Photograph by Alastair Thain

bio

BORN: Paris, France
August 18, 1933

> Polanski's mother died in a Nazi concentration camp. He avoided capture and was educated at the film school in Lodz, Poland.
> The director's greatest critical and commercial successes were *Rosemary's Baby* (1968) and *Chinatown* (1974), which revitalized the film noir movement and earned Polanski an Academy Award nomination.

> In 1969, Polanski's wife, actress Sharon Tate, and several of their close friends were murdered by the so-called Manson family. Tate was eight months pregnant at the time.
> In 1977, more tragedy: Polanski was arrested and charged with the statutory rape of a 13-year-old girl. After first denying the charges, he entered a partial guilty plea. Free on bail, he fled to France.
> His film, *The Pianist*, won Academy Awards in 2002 for Best Director, Best Actor, and Best Adapted Screenplay. Polanski couldn't attend the awards, as he still faces criminal proceedings if he ever returns to the United States.

Phil Spector

First, I'd like to know what God sees when he takes LSD. And second, I'd like to know what you say to God when he sneezes.

I wonder how Michael Jackson started out as a black man and ended up as a white girl. But in a world where carpenters get resurrected, anything is possible.

I am dysfunctional by choice, and I love my attitude problem.

If you talk to God, you're praying. If God talks back, it's schizophrenia.

I am constantly trapped in my own freedom, environment, and heredity.

I prefer life on the outskirts of hell, located east of a rock and west of a hard place. And since we're all, in reality, living in God's waiting room, I'm okay where I'm at.

Old age is anyone twenty-five years older than I am.

It does seem a pity that Noah and his party didn't miss the boat. That rather pessimistic outlook is endorsed by such things as (a) it takes your enemy and your friend to hurt you—the one to slander you and the other to tell you about it; (b) most people should be obscene and not heard; (c) the main problem with the Christian Right is that it is neither.

One positive thing about old age is that you can remember everything that happened, even if it didn't happen.

Today I find my life in a gloomy region, where the year is divided into one day and one night and lies entirely outside the stream of history. The purity of the air is without doubt due to the fact that the people around me have their windows closed. However, I guess my life is better than that of a poor, thin, spasmodic, hectic, shrill, and pallid being.

It's easy to understand God as long as you don't have to explain him.

I continue to try to live up to the standard of one of my heroes, Henry VIII, who perhaps came as close to the ideal of perfect wickedness as the infirmities of human nature will allow.

I've bought myself a beautiful and enchanting castle in a hick town where there is no place to go that you shouldn't go. I decided to move out of my other place, the Tarantula Arms, where I had a nice furnished web. It was located in Pasadena.

If I owned both hell and Pasadena, I'd sell Pasadena and live in hell.

Now that the impeachment nonsense has faded into history, I wouldn't mind getting my hands on that bloated, sexist, prissy, pompous, unsmiling, and thinking accuser and huge bantam cock of a man, Henry Hyde, who offers the quintessential proof that it is far better to keep your mouth shut and let everyone think you're stupid than to open it and leave no doubt.

There is nothing more terrifying than ignorance in action.

If the average man is made in God's image, then Mozart was plainly superior to God.

Love is an obsessive delusion that is cured by marriage.

The dread of loneliness is greater than the fear of bondage, so we get married.

bio

BORN: Bronx, New York
December 5, 1940

> In the early 1960s, Spector produced 20 hit singles in three years' time, working with such artists as the Crystals, Ben E. King, and the Righteous Brothers, whose "You've Lost That Lovin' Feeling" sold over two million copies.
> Spector created the famous "Wall of Sound," a milestone in recording history. The technique involved overdubbing instruments (five or six guitars, three or four pianos, a symphony of percussion) to create a massive roar.
> He was inducted into the Rock and Roll Hall of Fame in 1989.
> In 2003, Spector was charged with the murder of B-movie actress Lana Clarkson.

In my next life, I want to come back as either a proctologist, so I can deal with all the assholes I meet, or as a matador, so I can deal with all the bullshit.

Oh, I almost forgot. Bill Bailey just called and said he's not coming home.

Great minds discuss ideas, average minds discuss events, and small minds discuss people.

Since I'm one of those people who are not happy unless they are not happy, it's comforting to know that mental health doesn't always mean being happy. If it did, nobody would qualify.

Photograph by Mary Ellen Mark

J. Craig Venter

I wouldn't have mapped the human genome if I was lacking in confidence.

I've always had the notion that I would have an extraordinary life. Some people call that delusions of grandeur.

Luck favors the prepared mind.

It's unequivocally clear that life begins at birth and ends at death. And if most of the people on this planet understood that, they would lead their lives very differently. We always try to find religious or mysterious forces to fill in for our inadequacies, but heaven and hell are both here on earth every day, and we make our lives around them.

Everybody, unless they have money to give them independence, has to put up with an awful lot of bullshit.

In Vietnam, I saw people who gave up on life and died, and I saw other people who had no chance to live, yet did. The human spirit is a very powerful entity.

I got so depressed in Vietnam that I decided that I didn't want to live anymore. So I swam out into the ocean as far as I could, and I got out there in the middle of all these sharks and barracuda and sea snakes, and I thought, What the fuck am I doing out here? I turned around and swam back as fast as I could. That was one of the most profound moments in my life.

A lot of people—given my circumstances—would've ended up in prison or a mental institution or at the bottom of the ladder.

My father worked incredibly hard his whole life and was thinking about early retirement so he could start enjoying life more, and then he died. He was three years older than I am now. So I didn't make any plans of getting to this age. I didn't count on it.

It's easier to keep doing what you're doing than to go out and risk losing everything trying to do something new.

Trying to run your life over again is like trying to run the giant experiment of evolution over again. You can run the same experiment a thousand times and never get the same outcome, the same answer.

I usually internalize anger and try to turn it into constructive energy. I don't hold grudges. I'm not a vindictive person.

If we had an intelligent government, they'd be dealing with environmental problems now instead of trying to protect the industries that are causing the problems.

Fame is an intrinsic negative. People respond to you based on their preconceived notion of you, and that puts you at a continual disadvantage.

Life on this planet could have easily come from somewhere else, and it most likely did.

I can apparently deal with more independent variables than most people.

There is no thrill like planning something like this, going after it, and succeeding. It's a very selfish thing.

I wouldn't be me if I eliminated all the grief and unhappiness and bitterness in my life.

You can't just live in a comfortable little suburban neighborhood and get your education from movies and television and have any perspective on life.

When I'm in airports and crowds and foreign countries, I try to imagine the differences in the genetic codes of people. And I'm stunned how few differences there would be.

I have the potential for an addictive personality. My great-grandfather was killed at a young age by driving a horse and carriage at extremely high speeds while extremely inebriated. He fell off and was run over by his own carriage.

If people paid more attention to themselves and their own emotional well-being, all of society would be better for it.

I wish I knew then what I know now. I would've gotten far more chicks.

INTERVIEWED BY WIL S. HYLTON // Photograph by Nick Ruechel

bio

BORN: Salt Lake City, Utah
October 14, 1946

> After a stint in the Navy in the 1960s, Venter earned a Ph.D. in physiology and pharmacology.

> In 1999, he made headlines around the world when he announced that he had mapped the human genome.
> He is the former president and founder of Celera Genomics and, more recently, the president of the Center for the Advancement of Genomics.
> Venter was voted *Time* magazine's Person of the Year in 2000.

The Showmen

Yogi Berra

Rodney Dangerfield

George Foreman

Roy Jones Jr.

Garry Shandling

Donald Trump

Yogi Berra

I never go to the track. I don't like horses. They take too long.

Ask questions. Maybe it might lead to somethin'.

I'm lucky. Usually you're dead to get your own museum, but I'm still alive to see mine.

New York is *always* the place to play.

If I didn't make it in baseball, I won't have made it workin'. I didn't like to work.

I was the baby. My oldest brother was the best ballplayer of all of us. You ask anybody on the Hill in St. Louis—he was the best ballplayer on the Hill. My brother Lefty, he could hit. Man, he could hit.

I told my dad, "Dad, you realize if your other two sons had played ball, you'da been a millionaire." He said, "Blame your mother."

I was playin' American Legion Baseball. Bobby Hofman, used to play with the Giants, we were on the same team. We never had dugouts. We're sittin' on the ground. I always had my legs crossed and my arms folded. Bobby said, "You look like a yogi." And it stuck.

You don't have to swing hard to hit a home run. If you got the timing, it'll go.

I don't blame the players today for the money. I blame the owners. They started it. They wanna give it to 'em? More power to 'em.

It don't have to be a perfect pitch. If you see it good, swing at it. But if you can't hit it, lay off it.

My wife, she calls me Yogi. If she calls me Lawrence, I know she's mad at me.

The Hill was a good neighborhood. We all knew when to come in. They had a 4:30 whistle. We were playin' outside on the street, that 4:30 whistle blow, everybody drops everything, go and get that pail, get that can of beer for your father, put it on that table. They come home from work, they're thirsty.

For Christmas, I asked my dad, "I want a baseball bat, a glove, and a ball." He said, "Which one of the three do ya want?"

I had two pitchers go and hit me 'cause I hit 'em good. Gary Bell said, "You hit me too good, dago." He just called me that—I didn't mind. It wasn't mean. I know he didn't mean that. He was a good buddy of mine is why. He wouldn't throw at my head—you know, in the ass. Same way with Dizzy Trout. He said, "You hit me too good. I gotta get ya." Nothin' regular. Just for the heck of it.

When I caught, I'd look at the hitter, the way he strides. He strides in, then ya get the ball inside to him. I watched 'em pretty good.

Joe was the best player I ever saw. He didn't do anything wrong. DiMaggio I never saw slide. He just was there. It's funny—I never seen him slide for a ball. He run the bases good. Every damn thing. Never seen him without a tie. Always a dark-blue suit. *Sharp.* He come from the sticks, too.

A lot of guys go, "Hey Yog, say a Yogi-ism." I tell 'em, "I don't know any." They want me to make one up. I don't make 'em up. I don't even know when I say it. They're the truth. And it is the truth. I don't know.

Casey used to say, "When you're on first base and you go back to the bag, step on the guy's foot. Let him know you're there."

I get a kick out of some guys. They look at ya and say, "You look like Yogi Berra." I say, "Yeah, a lotta people tell me that." Then they say, "Ya can't be. *Can't* be." It's real funny. New York, they all know me, but when ya go in the airports, different towns, they look at ya—"You remind me of Yogi Berra."

I never figured I'd go into the Hall of Fame. A kid from the Hill.

INTERVIEWED BY SCOTT RAAB // Photograph by David Schuster

bio

BORN: St. Louis, Missouri
May 12, 1925

> Birth name: Lawrence Peter Berra
> The celebrated Yankees catcher played on fourteen pennant-winning teams and ten World Series champions during the 1940s and 1950s.
> Berra caught two no-hitters by Allie Reynolds in 1951. He also served as catcher during Don Larsen's perfect game in the 1958 World Series.
> He was voted "Most Valuable Player" by the American League three times (1951, 1954, 1955) and elected to the Baseball Hall of Fame in 1972.
> To the non-baseball crowd, Berra's sense of humor and gift for quirky phrasing made him a star. "Nobody goes there anymore, it's too crowded," "A nickel ain't worth a dime anymore," and "You can see a lot by observing" are just a few classic Yogi-isms.
> The Hanna-Barbera cartoon character, Yogi Bear, was named in his honor.

Rodney Dangerfield

(**Comedian**
Beverly Hills, California)

What good is being the best if it brings out the worst in you?

You know you're ugly when you go to the proctologist and he sticks his finger in your mouth.

I want a girl just like the girl that Dad kept on the side.

My childhood was bad. No father. Mother was greedy and brought me up awful—never made me breakfast once. I don't want to get started. One story is worse than another.

The only normal people are the ones you don't know too well.

People seldom live up to their baby pictures.

I've been writing jokes since I'm fifteen. Not out of happiness, but to go to a different place, because reality wasn't good to me.

A sense of humor is rare. It isn't telling a joke about how there are three ways to get to heaven. It's being in a restaurant and hearing someone say, "Everyone's got their tale of woe," and then turning around and saying, "Unfortunately, in life, there's more woe than tail."

I got my first break and became a singing waiter at eighteen or nineteen. I couldn't make a living at it. I quit. Then I got married and sold aluminum siding. My wife had problems physically. It was not good.

Never tell your wife she's lousy in bed. She'll go out and get a second opinion.

When I was forty, I was getting divorced, living in a low-class, dirty hotel in New York. My mother was dying of cancer. I owed $20,000. That was about the lowest. I came back to show business, and I couldn't get a job. I was turned down by every small-time agent in New York.

I started over again with an image: "Nothing goes right." Then when *The Godfather* came out, all I heard was, "Show respect.

BORN: Babylon, New York
November 22, 1921

> Birth name: Jacob Cohen
> Dangerfield got an audition to be on *The Ed Sullivan Show* by sneaking into a dress rehearsal; the appearance was his big break.
> He opened the famed Manhattan comedy club Dangerfield's in 1969; the club helped launch the careers of Tim Allen, Roseanne, Jerry Seinfeld, and Louie Anderson, among others.
> His film credits include starring roles in *Caddyshack* (1980), *Easy Money* (1983), and *Back to School* (1985), one of the first comedies to gross $100 million.
> He has been honored with a Grammy for his live comedy album *No Respect* (2000) and a Lifetime Creative Achievement Award from the American Comedy Awards. His trademark white shirt and red tie are on permanent display at the Smithsonian.

With me, you show respect." So I changed the image to "I don't get no respect." I tried it out in Greenwich Village. I remember the first joke I told: "Even as a kid, I'd play hide and seek and the other kids wouldn't even look for me." The people laughed. After the show, they started saying to me, "Me, too—I don't get no respect." I figured, let's try it again.

I can't figure women out. They put on makeup for three hours. They wear things that make them smaller. Things that make them bigger. Then they meet a man and they want truth.

It would be great if people never got angry at someone for doing something they've done themselves.

If sex is a pain in the ass, then you're doing it wrong.

After I got divorced, I said to myself, I will never, ever get married again. It was in cement. I went through a really rough twenty-five years, but it happened again. I fell in love. I told her, "Baby, I don't want a prenuptial agreement. This is it." Everyone told me I was nuts. Well, my new wife and I are married six years and we get along great. You can make anything work if you're both givers.

If every man was as true to his country as he was to his wife, we'd be in a lot of trouble.

Time and tide and hookers wait for no man.

It's great to have gray hair. Ask anyone who's bald.

If I could have dinner with anyone who lived in the history of the world, who would it be? That depends on the restaurant.

I'm a downer. I've been depressed my whole life. Figure it out.

He who laughs last didn't get it in the first place.

INTERVIEWED BY CAL FUSSMAN // **Photograph by Dan Winters**

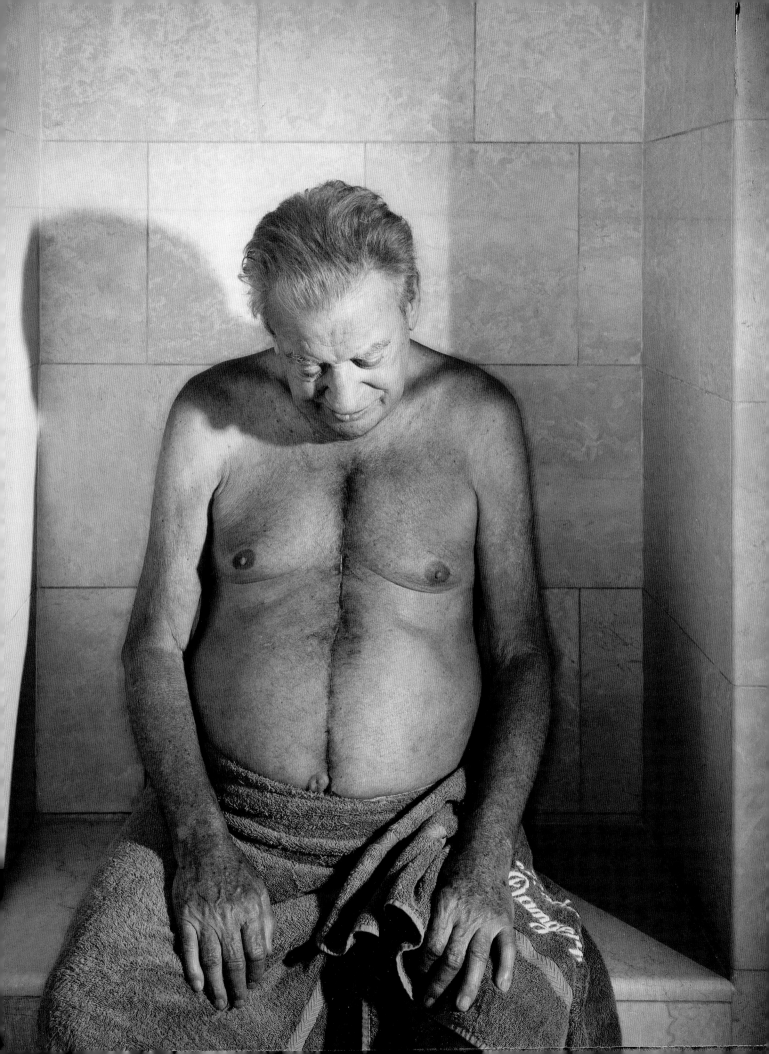

George Foreman

I dread handshakes. I've got some problems with my hands, and everywhere I go, people want to impress me with their grip. To make it worse, now *women* are coming up with that firm shake. So I'll say, "Gimme five!" If a boy wants a handshake, I'll just give him a hug.

I grew up in the Fifth Ward of Houston—the Bloody Fifth, we called it. Every weekend someone got killed.

When there was no lunch to take to school, I blew up a brown paper sack to make it look full.

Sometimes my older brothers and sisters would tease me, call me Mo-head. I didn't know why. Sometimes they'd say, "You're not really our brother." That would drive me crazy. Even before I outgrew them, they learned that the teasing wasn't worth the consequences.

I left school in eighth grade, ninth grade—something like that.

You don't know what it is to be heavyweight champ of the world until you become the heavyweight champ of the world. It's tough. You hear, "So-and-so became champ and he had five girls and five Cadillacs." So you get five Cadillacs and five girls just because so-and-so had it. It doesn't originate from you. It's not desire or physical urgency. It's all ignorance.

Most of us are just kids.

I remember how people looked at me as I left the United States for Zaire. "Man, that's George Foreman, going to fight Muhammad Ali." Then they'd drop their heads. Fear. Nobody would give me a straight-on look. It was a funny kind of admiration. There were people too scared to even ask for an autograph.

The day after I lost to Ali, people came by and put a hand on my shoulder and said, "It's okay, George. You'll have another chance." That was pity. From being feared to being pitied. Brother, that's a long fall.

I'll tell you how low a man can go. There was a B. B. King song that went, "Nobody loves me but my mother / And she could be jivin', too."

Evil lurks where disappointment lodges.

As an adult, I found out that my dad, J. D. Foreman, was not my biological dad. My mom and J. D. had broken up for a time, and that's when I was conceived. That's why my brothers and sisters called me Mo-head. What they were really saying was Moorehead. My biological dad was named Leroy Moorehead.

Changing your nature is the hardest thing to do. But I discovered that you can be who you choose to be.

Preaching is the most original thing I've ever done. There's nothing familiar about it. You have to be brave.

Losing your mother is the most mysterious lostness. You know how the astronauts walk in space, attached to the spacecraft by a line? The moment you find out your mother's died, you feel like someone's slipped the line off the craft. You're just floating away. Floating . . . floating . . . I remember my daughter called and said, "Don't you worry. I'm on my way." All the sudden that line snagged and I was anchored again.

Can't retire from exercising.

I called Muhammad the other day. I said, "Muhammad, I think I can really get you now in a rematch." And he said, "You crazy!" He doesn't speak rapidly, but he said, "George, I'm coming to see you." He said it with such love. No, I don't have any regrets.

The seventies are the best years. That's when you're wise.

My mother used to tell me, "You live and learn. Then you die and forget it all."

INTERVIEWED BY CAL FUSSMAN // Photograph by Dan Winters

bio

BORN: Marshall, Texas
January 10, 1949

> As an amateur heavyweight, Foreman won the Olympic gold medal in 1968. As a professional, he had 76 wins and 5 losses, with 68 wins by knockout.

> In 1974, Foreman lost his first fight. Muhammad Ali knocked him out in the eighth round of the "Rumble in the Jungle" in Zaire.

> Foreman is also known for his countertop grill, the George Foreman Lean Mean Grilling Machine, and as the spokesman for Meineke mufflers.

> He has five daughters and five sons. All of his sons are named George.

Roy Jones Jr.

Boxer
Pensacola, Florida

A man who ain't got no heart, you can't give him no heart.

All you got to do is say two words and I know if I wanna be around you.

You got a governor on your car, it ain't gonna go but so fast. All I got to do is get a car that can go faster than your car, and you will never beat me because that governor's gonna stop you at a certain speed. I know that, and you know that, too. So you're gonna quit.

One thing I learned from the '88 Olympics: It's not a question of if they *can* screw you over; it's a question of if they *will*. It's not the gold medal they took away from me. The medal doesn't mean anything. It's that they said I *lost*. That experience is well and alive in my mind.

Oscar De La Hoya can kiss my ass. The *Golden* Boy. Guaranteed, I'd beat him and two or three more of those motherfuckers in the same day.

I am just what they think I'm not. I'm that three times.

The night Marco Antonio Barrera got beaten by Junior Jones, I watched an HBO employee celebrate. He was yelling, "I told you! I told you! I can get *anybody* beat!" He didn't realize I caught him in the act. People can say whatever they want, but I saw it with my own eyes. They want your ass beat because upsets make news. News brings about excitement. And excitement brings about ratings. The objective is to bring you up to the tower and then tear your ass down. And if you don't believe that, you're crazy.

I saw a lot of guys with egos. They would try to hide something that ain't there. Then I would tear their asses up and they weren't the same no more. Ego can take you down if you get caught up in the hype.

If you're the champ, you're supposed to take whatever comes at you. If my opponents aren't good, it's not my fault.

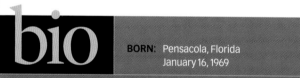

BORN: Pensacola, Florida
January 16, 1969

> As an amateur middleweight, Jones represented the United States at the 1988 Olympic Games in Seoul, Korea. As a professional, he has 49 wins and 1 loss, with 39 wins by knockout.
> Charismatic and flamboyant, Jones is credited with bringing the sport of boxing back from its post–Mike Tyson doldrums.
> Jones has enjoyed modest success in Hollywood, appearing in *The Matrix Reloaded* and several television shows, including *Average Joe*, *Beyond the Glory*, and *Married…with Children*.

I got real bored in '96. Wasn't nobody to fight. Nothing to look forward to. That's when I started playing basketball again. Had I not started playing basketball, my boxing career would have failed. But I went from a sport where nobody could touch me to another where I couldn't touch nobody. First time we'd play teams, guys would go by me and give me hell. Made me hustle twice as hard. As I got in the groove of it, these guys didn't get by me so easy. First time, yeah. Second time, maybe. Third time, it wasn't the same Roy Jones. Now they're saying, "Damn, you got so much better!" It made me see both sides. It taught me the difference between having the talent, being blessed, and working hard and not having the talent but having the guts and wanting to be the best. I could appreciate being at the top of my sport. At the time, I could be myself on the basketball court and know what would be coming at me in the ring. I know how that guy feels. I know what he's thinking. He ain't nobody, but he wants to make *me* look like a nobody. And that's what allows me to whup him so good.

People can look at you however they want. *You* gotta look at you.

My father didn't beat me up. It's just that sometimes you make mistakes; you gotta pay for them.

When I started, I knocked out about seventeen of 'em in a row. But I hurt people. That's not that good a way to be. I could fuck somebody up. I'm that strong. If I started showing people how mean I really am, somebody could wind up dead. If I fought like I was looking for a place in history, it would ruin me as a person. I don't think history is worth selling my soul. God wouldn't want me to be the type of rooster that kills another rooster. So I'm gonna chill and stay the nice guy that I am.

Everything's real cool now between my daddy and me. I'm a man, and he's a man. And we both understand that. I love my daddy to death. But he had to move to let me fly.

Always go back to where you started. That's the secret.

I ain't the toughest motherfucker in the world. I ain't Mr. Superman. Not trying to be Mr. Tough Guy. Don't want to be. Tell you one thing, though: I'm one of the smartest motherfuckers in the world. You've been talking to a fuckin' genius.

INTERVIEWED BY CAL FUSSMAN // Photograph by Martin Schoeller

Garry Shandling

Comedian, actor
Los Angeles

I'm more handsome than I act.

You're born a heterosexual. It's not a choice. Who would choose this? The guilt, the shame . . . and do you think I'm *happy* having to hire a decorator?

Call me old-school, but I miss the cold war.

Men who betray women also betray other men. Women shouldn't feel so special.

Gossip is a sin.

I started boxing for exercise, and on the very first day, the trainer got in the ring with me and said, "Whoever controls the breathing in the ring controls the fight." I immediately passed out.

I had a car accident when I was twenty-seven in which I was nearly killed. I had a vivid near-death experience that involved a voice asking, "Do you want to continue leading Garry Shandling's life?" Without thinking, I said, "Yes." Since then, I've been stuck living in the physical world while knowing, without a doubt, that there's something much more meaningful within it all. That realization is what drives my life and work.

Dating a professional actress is tough. Especially if you're up for the same part.

Love is not enough to save a relationship.

My mother did the best she could. Sorry.

Dogs are not people. Be leery of any woman who refers to her dogs as her "kids," because you'll only end up paying for their schooling.

I remember when I was a struggling comic appearing for the first time in Las Vegas. Don Rickles came in to watch the new guy. Afterward, he came backstage, and I asked him if he thought I was funny. He said, "You *know* when you're funny. You don't have to ask." And he was right.

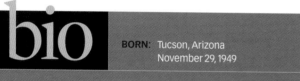

bio

BORN: Tucson, Arizona
November 29, 1949

> *The Larry Sanders Show* (HBO), Shandling's ingenious parody of television talk shows, won numerous Emmy Award nominations and CableAce awards in the 1990s.
> Shandling also had a four-year run with *It's Garry Shandling's Show,* which appeared on Fox.
> His film credits include *Comedian, Town & Country, What Planet Are You From?*, *Hurly Burly,* and *Love Affair.*

Dr. Phil is hiding something. Otherwise, why wouldn't he use his last name?

Everyone at a party is uncomfortable. Knowing that makes me more comfortable.

Nice guys finish first. If you don't know that, then you don't know where the finish line is.

Some people can fake it their whole lives.

I never listen to the audiotapes of my shrink sessions because the audience is usually so bad, I can't tell which jokes work and which ones don't.

Tom Hanks seems to know exactly what he's doing.

I once saw an elaborate landscape in a gallery, drawn in pencil, that took my breath away. Then I realized the artist probably didn't have enough confidence to use a pen.

A woman once asked me to autograph her T-shirt right across the chest. It only occurred to me later that she may have recognized me.

Nothing can succeed and last without teamwork.

I was anxious and depressed ahead of my time. I didn't need 9/11 to realize that in life, anything can happen. I've been on a state of alert since high school. Code plaid.

Impermanence. Impermanence. Impermanence.

Intellect without heart scares me.

Buddha didn't get married because his wife would have said, "What, are you going to sit around like that all day?"

I'll never agree to make another list like this one.

Photograph by Dan Winters

Donald Trump

Builder
New York City

The best thing I've ever done? Well, I've created four beautiful children. You mean, other than that?

My father was a builder in Brooklyn and Queens, a very smart businessperson who understood life. He taught me to keep my guard up. The world is a pretty vicious place.

My mom was a wonderful woman who was, in many ways, the opposite of my father. Very relationship oriented, very warm and open and generous to people. So I got different qualities from both. It was a great combination.

My life essentially is one big, fat phone call.

Hold on. Gotta take this one. . . . *Reeeeegis*, my man! How you doing? . . . The best pitcher in baseball going against us tonight. And Roger was great last time, but he's forty-one. Yeah, I'm going. Definitely. Are you? . . . *Ohhh!* . . . And you can't get out of it? . . . *Reeeeg!* You *can't* go see that! You can see that any night. This is a once-in-a-lifetime game. *Once in a lifetime!* You can't sit through a Broadway show with the Yankees playing the Red Sox in game seven! Go tomorrow night! Look, *I'll* get you a ticket. *Reeeeg! Reeeeeeeeeeg!* Look, even if you sit home and watch it on television, you're *not* gonna go to a Broadway show. . . . If you change your mind, let me know. I love you, darling. Take care. Be good.

That was Regis.

The most important things in life are your relationships and your health.

For me, business comes easier than relationships.

The most I've ever asked the bank for? The job I'm building on the West Side is a $4 billion to $5 billion job.

bio

BORN: New York, New York
June 14, 1946

> Trump emerged as one of the most powerful real-estate moguls of the '80s; his properties included the Trump Tower, the Trump Parc, the Plaza Hotel, and the New Jersey Generals.
> Forced to declare bankruptcy in 1990, he bounced back by the end of the decade.
> He is co-producer of NBC's reality show *The Apprentice*, in which 16 contestants vie for a position at one of Trump's corporations.
> Trump has been married to (and divorced from) Ivana Trump and Marla Maples.

Work hard to take the gamble out of the gamble.

Going through tough times is a wonderful thing, and everybody should try it. Once.

I was walking down Fifth Avenue with Marla Maples in 1991. This was at the peak of the bad market. Across the street I saw a man in front of Tiffany with a tin cup. I looked at Marla and said, "You know, right now that man is worth $900 million more than I am." When I told Marla this, she didn't run away. Of course, I would have saved a little money if she had.

I had a lot of friends who went bankrupt and you never hear from them again. I worked harder than I'd ever worked getting myself out of it. Now my company is much bigger than it was in the eighties—many times. The Guinness Book of Records gave me first place for the greatest financial comeback of all time.

Fighting for the last penny is a very good philosophy to have.

My children have shown me that they are willing to work hard to become successful. That's very important. Because when children grow up in wealth, you always have doubts.

I learned a lot from my brother Fred's death. He was a great-looking guy. He had the best personality. He had everything. But he had a problem with alcohol and cigarettes. He knew he had the problem, and it's a tough problem to have. He was ten years older than me, and he would always tell me not to drink or smoke. And to this day I've never had a cigarette. I've never had a glass of alcohol. I won't even drink a cup of coffee. I just stay away from those things because he had such a tremendous problem. Fred did me a great favor. It's one of the greatest favors anyone's ever done for me.

If you don't have an understanding of your opponent, things aren't going to work out very well for you.

CEO compensation has gotten outrageous. Some of these guys come into these big, monster, powerful companies, and all of a sudden they're making $40, $50, $60 million a year. It's one thing if you create a company and you start from scratch. But some of these companies have been around for a hundred years. You increase the price of a bottle of ketchup by one penny and you look like a genius. It seems ridiculous. The solution? Have the people who own the stock vote on it.

A bus coming from a church in Louisiana gets wiped out. It's a difficult thing to figure. You would think that a bus coming from a church would be absolutely protected. But it wasn't. You look at what's going on in the world and you say, Boy, God has to be pretty tough.

Has sex changed over time? Not that I've noticed. I hope I can say that in fifteen years.

I nod, and it is done.

INTERVIEWED BY CAL FUSSMAN // Photograph by Michael Edwards

The Interviewers

Many journalists have conducted "What I've Learned" interviews over the years, but Esquire's writers-at-large are responsible for the vast majority. In lieu of a traditional "about-the-author" blurb, we've asked them to share what they've learned from "What I've Learned."

Cal Fussman

Writer, Chapel Hill, North Carolina
BORN: November 16, 1956

Never trust a man who doesn't like watermelon.

If sex is a pain in the ass, you're doing it wrong. Rodney Dangerfield taught me that.

At work there's always one person higher than you in the pecking order who's a complete asshole.

I haven't watched more than an episode or two of any television series since 1973. I've survived.

When interviewing somebody, use two tape recorders loaded with fresh batteries. That way you can relax.

When listening to somebody, look him in the eye as if he is the only person in the world.

A wise man knows what he says. A fool says what he knows. I got that from a fortune cookie.

When in a doughnut-eating competition, press down hard on each one before biting into it. If you don't, the air inside will bloat your belly and you'll get blown out of the race after six.

You can count all the seeds in an apple, but you can't count all the apples in a seed.

When I was about twenty-three, I left my job and took off with a backpack on an around-the-world trip. A friend who hated his job was envious. "It's very easy," I told him. "Just buy yourself a ticket and get your ass on a plane." He shook his head. "I'd love to but I can't. I'm afraid that when I come back home, I won't be able to find another job." So he stayed at his job, and he most assuredly hates it to this day.

If you sleep less than you need, you'll be tired. If you sleep more than you need, you'll be depressed. It's crucial to sleep not a minute more or less than necessary.

If you see the bind you're in as bad luck, you're helpless. If you see it as a challenge to be overcome, you're empowered.

Laughter is not only great medicine but great food, too.

Know the rules so you can break them properly.

When personal survival is concerned, art has no value. As far as art is concerned, personal survival has no value.

Age has no number. Ray Arcel, the boxing cornerman, passed that on.

We cannot solve our problems with the same thinking we used when we created them. Albert Einstein got that right.

Respect the ocean.

Put a comma in the wrong place and the whole sentence is fucked up.

My firstborn son taught me in an hour what my father tried to impart in twenty-one years.

When I was a young aspiring writer, I drove more than a thousand miles to meet the author Harry Crews. He had no idea who I was or why I was coming. But I'd been overwhelmed by one of his books, and I just got in my car and fifteen hours later I was in Gainesville, Florida, knocking on the partly open front door of his home. There was no answer. I knocked some more. After a few minutes, I walked inside. Hell, I didn't drive a thousand miles for nothing. And there was Harry, laid out on a chair with an empty bottle of booze on his chest. As I got closer, his eyes opened, and without a question he welcomed me. He told me to go down to Gator Gulch and fill a cardboard box with liquor. So I did. We got to drinking and talking, and the more he drank, the more lucid he became. It was absolutely amazing—although it may have just seemed that way because I was getting hammered. I don't recall much of what happened as the evening progressed, but I do remember asking him if he kept a diary. "How can you remember everything?" I wondered, meaning, "How can you remember anything when you're constantly fucked up?" He looked me in the eye and said, "The good shit sticks." I've never forgotten that, nor kept a diary since.

I once saw a letter written by Nelson Mandela. There was no letterhead bearing the presidential seal of South Africa or anything else at the top of the page. The letter was simply handwritten on a blank piece of paper and signed "Mandela." That's power.

A great editor can help make ten great writers. But a hundred great writers can't make a good editor.

Tom Junod

Writer, Atlanta, Georgia
BORN: April 9, 1958

I grew up in Wantagh, New York. There was paneling in my room. The knots in one piece of paneling looked just like eyes. And once when I was in high school, I looked at those eyes and thought, "That's what God looks like, man." I still think so, sort of.

Proof that God exists: fruit. I mean, it's so good. And it's for us, you know?

I'd love to play hip-hop for Shakespeare. He'd either wiggle his skinny arse, or he'd puke. And then we'd know where our civilization stands.

I live in a suburb of Atlanta. You hear people say that humans are still going to be around in sixty thousand years. I'm like, "Hey, man, I live in Atlanta. You think Atlanta's gonna be around in sixty thousand years?"

I don't want to meet Elvis Costello. I just want to look at him. He is almost as scary as Chuck Berry.

I have a pit bull. His name is Carson. People say he must be named after Carson Daly, he's so sweet. I say no. He's named after Tom Carson. The only movies he likes are from the Farrelly Brothers.

I used to sell handbags. Long time ago, now. I had a crazy boss. He had the narrowest feet I ever saw. 13AAA. It was like walking around on needle-nosed pliers. He used to go nuts, if ladies called them "purses." He'd fulminate. "They're not purses, Ma'am. They're handbags. A purse is something you keep your coins in." I hated him. But he was right.

Coldest I've ever been? Wichita Falls, Texas. 1980. I was selling handbags. Daaaaaaamn. Don't ever let anyone tell you that Texas can't be cold.

Two of the guys I interviewed were named Chuck. What are the odds of that, man?

Scott Raab

Writer, Glen Ridge, New Jersey
BORN: August 6, 1952

You can't beat growing up in Cleveland. You learn to hope against hope. You grow to appreciate each gentle wind and ray of sun. And you prize every laugh—because you know in your soul that nothing you truly care about in life ends well.

Ike Turner is a sweet guy to talk to, but I wouldn't mess with him.

The older I get, the more I love baseball.

I've had professional intercourse with three supermodels—Rebecca Romijn, Christy Turlington, and Naomi Campbell. None of them was the least bit dumb, and each was a literally stunning physical presence. Still, I'd rather sit down with Yogi Berra. And I'd rather have sex with my wife. Not that any of 'em offered. Not even Yogi.

Hitler, Stalin, Pol Pot, sure. But when I get to Hell, I'd better see John Elway with a trident up his ass.

Ted Williams was loud, profane, and funny. He started yelling at me before he even came into the room, just to test me—the ultimate alpha male. He was nearly eighty then, and not in the best of shape, but he would've sat and talked baseball all day. I've never met a man more alive.

There are no tricks to writing, no tricks to love, no tricks to anything worth working at. If you think there are, you're a punk.

Lou Reed is supposed to be a tough interview, but he was very nice. The best part for me was recalling all the times I saw him perform in and around Cleveland back in the early and mid-seventies, and realizing that this was the first time I had ever seen Lou without throwing up or getting into a car accident on my way home.

The smartest thing I ever did was get sober.

John H. Richardson

Writer, Katonah, New York
BORN: October 11, 1954

Decadent people are kind. Righteous people are cruel. But even though I've learned this lesson over and over again, I'm always a little scared when I meet someone like Larry Flynt or Roman Polanski.

Philip Johnson is famous for his glass house. But right behind it is a solid brick house without a single window, and nobody ever talks about that.

People need to tell their stories to someone who will write them down. It's almost a religious activity. That's why they get so mad if they think you got it wrong—you're not just a sloppy reporter, you're Satan. And they're right.

Even in Hollywood, there are very few cynical Machiavellian manipulators. Most people believe in what they do and are happy to explain it to you.

Maybe tolerance for ambiguity helps. Maybe an open mind helps. But the basic difference between a grandma and a grandpa and someone you'd want to hang out with is sex—if they're curious about it, talking about it, writing about it, making movies about it, they're alive. You could chart it on a graph.

Secrets are overrated. Usually the truth is right there on the surface, ignored.

Artists know a lot about one thing. Journalists know a little about many things. This can make communication difficult.

Everything contains its opposite. There's a pervert in every holy man and a fascist in every libertarian. And vice versa. It's not hypocrisy, it's human nature.

At some point, you have to stop and think. But not too soon!

Mike Sager

Writer, La Jolla, California
BORN: August 17, 1956

Writing is editing.

What you say and do are equally important.

Most people put on their pants one leg at a time.

Hate is fear. Fear is insecurity.

Win by example.

Your wife is always right.

Hard work pays good dividends.

My great-grandfather sold rags and I can, too.

There's no place like home.

Respect must be earned.

Be number one in a class of one.

Do unto others as you would have them do unto you.

God helps those who help themselves.

Editors are nurturers. A good one is hard to find.

I have always depended upon the kindness of strangers.

Less is more.

Photo Credits

Photo Credits: Front Cover

Index of the Interviews